Monumental
NEW YORK!

The Crown Point Lighthouse, Crown Point, NY.

Monumental NEW YORK!

A GUIDE TO 30 ICONIC MEMORIALS IN UPSTATE NEW YORK

CHUCK D'IMPERIO

SYRACUSE UNIVERSITY PRESS

ISBN: 978-0-8156-0962-9

Library of Congress Cataloging-in-Publication Data
D'Imperio, Chuck.
Monumental New York! : a guide to 30 iconic memorials in upstate New York /
Chuck D'Imperio.
p. cm.
ISBN 978-0-8156-0962-9 (pbk. : alk. paper)
1. Memorials—New York (State)—Guidebooks.   2. Historic sites—New York (State)—
Guidebooks.   3. New York (State)—Guidebooks.   I. Title.
F120.D56 2011
974.7—dc23   2011017641

Manufactured in the United States of America

Monumental New York! is dedicated to Frances and Katie D'Imperio, two little girls who went with their Dad on a hundred trips around the state, looking up statues, memorials, and gravestones. I'm so proud of the way you've grown into such beautiful young women. I wouldn't trade the times we had in the car together for anything.

CHUCK D'IMPERIO is a longtime radio broadcaster at Central New York Radio Group's station WDOS in Oneonta, helming his top-rated morning show since 1989. He was inducted into the New York State Country Music Hall of Fame as New York State's Broadcaster of the Year, 2000.

Chuck is the author of several books about his native Upstate New York region, including *My Town Is a Cathedral: My Memories of Sidney*; *Upstate New York: History Happened Here*; and *Great Graves of Upstate New York: The Final Resting Places of 70 True American Legends*. His bi-monthly newspaper column entitled *I Was Just Thinking* appears in the *Oneonta Daily Star*. He is also a popular public speaker. Chuck can be reached at UpstateBooks@yahoo.com.

Chuck D'Imperio is married to Trish, and they are the parents of Frances, Katie, Abby, and Joey. They live, of course, in Upstate New York.

CONTENTS

FOREWORD

JAMES L. SEWARD

*U*pstate New York's history brims with famous events, renowned men and women, and unprecedented discoveries. From the 1600s when Henry Hudson sailed our waters on an exploratory voyage, to 1788 when we joined the Union as the eleventh state, to the legend of Abner Doubleday's fabled discovery of baseball, our national pastime, the Empire State has witnessed a vast array of life-altering moments. Fortunately, many of these history-making figures and occurrences are permanently etched in time through wonderfully distinct monuments, statues, and memorials dotting our upstate landscape.

As a state senator, I have had the privilege of traveling throughout New York and witnessing many of these celebrated historical markers firsthand. These brilliant testaments serve as a connection to our state's past and an artful reminder of the state's proud foundation. Now through *Monumental New York!* you too can take this spellbinding journey.

This new volume by flourishing author Chuck D'Imperio chronicles thirty select monuments and the unique story purveyed by each. The book provides the reader with factual descriptions and well-researched information, but it is so much more than a straightforward reference guide or directory. By flipping through the pages within, one can travel across Upstate New York and truly experience the sights that make the region such a unique and special place.

D'Imperio acts as your personal tour guide, detailing not only the particulars of each historical tribute but also the human interest characteristics and, in many cases, untold stories behind the carved creations and their subjects. It is as if General Herkimer or the Sandlot Kid, two of the statues from my own senatorial district, have come to life to let us know why they have been immortalized in granite.

As a long-time radio host and newspaper columnist, D'Imperio has consistently offered a great appreciation for the Upstate region on full display in this book. A hall of fame broadcaster, "Big Chuck," as he is known to his loyal legion of listeners, has served as a constant beacon across an ever-changing medium. His exuberant and humorous style has provided information to the public, in some instances to purely entertain, in others to inform of local, regional, and global events, and in the most extreme situations to save lives.

In his previous writings D'Imperio has welcomed us to his hometown of Sidney, taken us to the final resting places of great American legends, and, most recently, transported us to the sites of significant events in Upstate's notable history. *Monumental New York!* extends the journey, introducing the reader to both the well-known and obscure statues and memorials, some in the center of town, others tucked away off rarely traveled thoroughfares.

I invite you to read about the wondrous monuments of Upstate New York and, if the mood strikes, to visit them yourself. Without a doubt, the words contained within will inspire many outings to the Capital District, the Hudson Valley, Western New York, the Finger Lakes, the Adirondacks, and my home region, Leatherstocking Country, as readers seek out these marvelous treasures. Enjoy Upstate New York and enjoy *Monumental New York!*

(Editor's note: James L. Seward is a senator from the Fifty-first Senatorial District, New York State.)

MY MONUMENTAL JOURNEY

I have always loved statues, monuments, and memorials. Okay, not *always*, but for a very long time!

I grew up in a pretty little town called Sidney, which hugs the banks of the Susquehanna River, near the geographic center of New York State. Our town is a factory town (magnetos and calendars), and other than being a great place to grow up and become a factory worker or a shopkeeper, well, nothing *really* important ever happened there. Sidney has no statues, monuments, or memorials to marvel at. (We did have a couple of very impressive Civil War cannons in the cemetery until they disappeared a few years back.) So in 1967 when I left for college in the big city of Albany, I not only became the first male in my long family line to go off to college, but I also stepped through the looking glass into a world of wonder, amazement, and urban fascination.

Having never been exposed to the nuances of public art before, I was now confronted with a wonderful world of majestic rearing equestrian memorials honoring ancient wartime leaders, emotional tributes to deceased local heroes, and curious monuments to long-forgotten events. Albany had them all, and I loved each and every one of them.

I have always been fascinated by the beauty, originality, history, and craftsmanship of the thousands of monuments that dot our countryside. I am not an art student or a design expert. I have no real knowledge of the craft of monument making. But I have been inextricably drawn to them over the years, for both their historic importance and noteworthiness. Whether I come across a so-and-so was born here plaque on the side of an old building or a towering bronze figure of a long-forgotten military hero, I always stop, look, and absorb.

A few monuments, from various times and places in my life, have stayed with me all these years, and I would like to tell you about them. I do this to explain how

I became interested in the statues, monuments, and memorials that are seemingly everywhere and to illustrate how this fascination led to the writing of this book.

In 1967, I graduated from high school and enrolled in college at Albany Business College. A classic fish out of water, I was completely entranced by the whirl of urban life. My first walks around Albany were awesome.

The majestic New York State Capitol, the construction hurly-burly in the South End (the grand Empire State Plaza was just being built and was only a gleam in Rocky's eye), stunning Washington Park (right out my back door), dramatic State Street careening straight downhill from the capitol onto the doorstep of the mammoth, gargoyled, Europeanesque D&H Railroad Building—it was all a real eye-opener for me, to say the least.

The first great monument that I really was taken with (or really *saw*) in Albany was right there, out my back door, in Washington Park. It was a Bible-themed depiction of Moses on top of a rocky mount. Not knowing its official name, I called it Moses on the Rockpile. It was enormous and impressive and it mesmerized me. I spent many days (and nights) there, sitting under the towering elm trees, whiling away my free time, in the shadow of my friend Moses.

It was a statuary beacon, beckoning me to come and visit. Like a siren's call, it magnetically drew me to this beautiful spot in this famous place. My school chum Steve Wade and I would walk the paths of Washington Park endlessly, stroll its iron bridges, explore the environs of its ancient boathouse, and share our nineteen-year-old dreams. They were wonderful times, in a new magical place, and those days and nights usually ended up with the sun coming up over Moses. As Albany was my first city, Moses on the Rockpile was my first introduction to the world of public art, and though I have traveled far and wide and researched and written much, that curious memorial in my backyard park remains my greatest and sentimental favorite monument.

By 1971, I had moved to New York City. Not having much money to splurge during my Gotham Days I never went to the ultimate monument of them all, the Statue of Liberty. But I did wander the sidewalks of New York and really enjoyed the monuments that I came upon.

The groaning Atlas and the deific Prometheus at Rockefeller Center were big favorites of mine. They seemed so out of place in such a beehive of activity. Standing solidly, silently, and stoically amid the squealing children on the skating rink and the shoulder-to-shoulder sidewalk vendors, the two towering giants always conveyed an appearance of great sadness to me. Joan of Arc atop her charging steed in Riverside Park is one of the greatest equestrian statues. And Christopher Columbus standing guard over his circle from his perch sixty-nine feet above the tumult was much enjoyed by this kid whose last name has two capital letters, an apostrophe, *and* a vowel at the end. *La bella, magnifica statua!*

Today, my trips to New York are more frequent than ever. But old habits die hard, and I still look for and enjoy my favorite statuary memories from the past. And I add to them. Alice in Wonderland and Hans Christian Anderson in Central Park are always voted among the most beloved pieces of public art in the city, but even though the park offers all the iconic treats imaginable (from Balto the hero dog to William Shakespeare) my favorite is still the first statue commissioned for the park. The Indian Hunter, by John Quincy Adams Ward, shows a young Native American hunter and his dog peering into the unknown from atop a giant boulder. It has a certain rugged majesty to it.

New favorites crowd my list of monuments to revisit, too. The beautiful statue of Mahatma Gandhi at the United Nations, the impossibly sad Irish Hunger Memorial near Ground Zero, and John Lennon's touching Imagine at Strawberry Fields are relatively new New York favorites of mine. And I must admit I am still drawn to the colossal Botero nudes, Adam and Eve, still reliably at their posts in the lobby of the new Time Warner Center at Columbus Circle. These cheeky, Macy's Thanksgiving Day bronze balloons stand shyly aloof, determinedly displaying all of their shortcomings to the world around them.

Ever since my Albany days, I have enjoyed seeking out and researching the statues, monuments, and memorials wherever I was living or traveling at the time. In the mid-1970s I visited Pamplona, Spain, for the ritual running of the bulls (no, I didn't run). Ernest Hemingway put this city and festival on the map in his 1926 book *The Sun Also Rises,* but I discovered it in what turned out to be a life-changing book for me, James Michener's *The Drifters* (1971). Although the eight drifters in the book ended up in the Spanish Costa del Sol city of Torremolinos, the entire region referred to in Michener's tome fascinated me, which resulted in my visit to the Feast of San Fermin in Pamplona.

In July 1975, I and five of my own drifting compatriots pulled into this sun-baked city in our orange Volkswagen bus. The city was teeming with thousands of visitors from all over the world. The revelry that ensued over the next several days was of mythic proportions, all culminating in the mayhem that *is* the running of the bulls. While I was completely immersed in this dazzling bacchanalia, I felt the siren's call again to another monument: the famous bust of Ernest Hemingway.

The bust stands in the Plaza de Toros, at the end of the bulls' route through the city. I was completely drawn to it, much as he must have been drawn to this exotic place decades before. This large, boxy, robust portrayal of the writer gazes out at the crowds swarming into the bullfighting arena. Hundreds of red scarves adorned and littered the statue, tokens from the runners and participants of the previous day's run. Young people sat in the shadow of Hemingway, sharing warm wine squirted out of sheepskin bladders; others dozed at the writer's feet or read (or pretended to read) dog-eared copies of classic Basque literature. Everyone who passed by touched the statue for good luck, so much so that the stone appeared to be disintegrating a bit from all the attention. I too placed my red scarf around Hemingway's neck for luck. When I did this I thought I was about as far from little Sidney, New York, as anybody my age could get!

I have vivid memories of those warm days along the Mediterranean coast and the craziness of the Feast of San Fermin, but none are more vivid than my memories of the monument in the plaza and how I felt so inextricably connected to it. I bonded with that statue so far from home, and yes, I drank wine squirted into my mouth by a lovely young girl from Greece, I read (or tried to read) Miguel de Unamuno y Jugo's Basque classic *Paz en la Guerra*, and then, ultimately, I fell solidly asleep at the feet of Papa Hemingway. It was wonderful.

<hr />

Around 1975, I moved to Los Angeles. In the first week there, I read an article that got me interested in the monuments in the City of Angels. I followed the story, which led me to the most unusual monument I have ever come across. The facts were bizarre.

A 116-ton boulder had rolled off the Malibu coastline and had landed like a giant elephant smack dab in the middle of the Pacific Coast Highway. It was immovable. Engineers had been called in to study the best way to get rid of this obstacle, traffic slowed as travelers were routed around the giant rock, and it was a major news story for a week or so. Finally, an unknown Australian named Brett-Livingstone Strong stepped forward and offered to buy the boulder for $100. He hauled this piece of a mountain onto a flatbed truck and dragged it to Hollywood (where else!) where he plunked it down in front of the giant complex known as Century City. There, Strong, a sculptor, began to create an homage to one of America's greatest icons, actor John Wayne. He used chainsaws and jackhammers and invited the public to come to Century City and view the creation of the John Wayne Boulder.

Since I had no job yet, I did just that. For days I took the bus to the shopping mall at the base of the giant towers in Century City and watched as this youthful artisan created the most amazing bust of the Duke. Eventually the crowds grew larger and more enthusiastic as Wayne's crooked grin and tall Stetson hat took shape. When it was completed it was hailed as a great triumph for the city—and the sculptor—and it graced the entrance to the complex for the year after its completion. I found myself drawn to the idea of public art being a symbiotic connection between populace and substance. It was, after all, just a great big stupid 116-ton rock that fell off a cliff. But it morphed into something far more than that under the gentle hands of the air hammer–wielding Strong. Today, decades later, I feel a kinship to that boulder, to John Wayne, to Century City, and even to Brett-Livingstone Strong, whom I watched but never met. And when he sold his John Wayne monument to an Arizona investor for more than a million dollars, I cheered him for his showmanship!

The end of the seventies found me living in Houston. It is the most muscular and manly "art town" I have ever been in. I fell in love with a monument both quintessentially Texan and nationally historic. My brother Jim and his beautiful wife Sandy, a native Texan ("Chuck, y'all just gonna *luv* it here!") put me up for a spell in 1979 in Houston. I remember the day they took me out to the San Jacinto Battlefield to show me (in Sandy's words), "the birthplace of *our* Texas." The site is just east of the city, along a meandering river known locally as "the ship channel." It is hallowed ground to Texans and one of the most amazing marriages I have seen between a historic place and an equally historic monument.

On April 21, 1836, Sam Houston and 910 of his men routed a much larger Mexican army at this riverside swamp, at last giving Texas its independence. Despised General Antonio Lopez de Santa Anna was captured and a surrender was enacted. The Texans had screamed their way into the unsuspecting Mexican camp at daybreak, under the calls to "Remember Goliad!" and "Remember the Alamo!" (two infamous defeats at the hands of Santa Anna). The Mexican army suffered heavy casualties, but Houston's troops suffered only lightly. The importance of this battle cannot be understated. How then, a century later, would they honor and memorialize something on such a grand scale?

As Jim and Sandy and I drove up the long winding road to the battlefield, I was asking myself exactly that. Soon, on the horizon, the answer became abundantly clear to me. They memorialized it the only way they can: Texas style!

The San Jacinto Monument is a 570-foot pile of pure, unadulterated Texas. The tallest, heaviest war memorial *in the world*, it is fifteen feet taller than the Washington Monument. Some of Texas's greatest engineers, including the legendary Jesse H. Jones, oversaw the construction of this obelisk, the largest memorial construction project up to that time. It was so huge that to fill in just the foundation of the obelisk, fifty-seven hours of a steady pour of concrete had to take place. It is the largest Art Deco object ever built, and like the purest dictate of the Art Deco style, one's eyes are fixed at the sleek lines, rising from the ground, until you are justly rewarded at the top. And what a Texas-size reward it is! Atop the monument sits a massive, 220-ton Star of Texas made out of steel, wire, and stone.

Texas is full of great monuments from Beaumont to El Paso to Dallas and to Galveston. But for me the eyes of Texas will always shine the brightest along the muddy ship channel just east of Houston, where a giant cement spire pointing to the sky reminds me of my time spent in this most unforgettable place.

<hr>

As an inveterate road warrior, I am always pleased to commit to memory some of the great statues, monuments, and memorials I stumble upon while seeing the United States.

One favorite that has stayed with me over the years is the Civil Rights Memorial in Montgomery, Alabama. I did not know of the existence of the Civil Rights Memorial until I arrived in the city. Designed by young Maya Lin, who also created the haunting Vietnam Veterans Memorial in Washington, DC, this simple, eloquent, and moving pedestal of still water is inscribed in gold with the names of forty civil rights martyrs who were murdered between 1954 and 1968. The visitor is drawn into the memorial space and the pedestal itself, and when a hand is thrust into the still pool of invisible water, ripples disrupt the entire memorial, making it a personally startling experience. The first name is Rev. George Lee, one of the first black people to register to vote in Mississippi, who was murdered on May 7, 1955, and the final name is the civil rights leader Rev. Martin Luther King Jr., who was murdered on April 4, 1968.

I have witnessed many memorials to the Holocaust around the country and admired the sad eloquence of all of them. For me, however, the most unforgettable one is in Boston, a city I have spent much time in.

Located near the gift shops, tourist attractions, and Irish pubs of lively center city Boston (near Hanover and North Streets), the memorial rises unobtrusively along a grassy area paralleling the sidewalk. You almost don't realize it is there until you are actually in it. The monument consists of a series of glass towers, each representing one of the large Nazi death camps. You walk through these towers until you slowly realize that the numbers etched along the glass panels are ID numbers from concentration camp prisoners, and the names and quotes from along the walkway are from survivors and writers. As you walk from glass tower to glass tower (from camp to camp) you slowly, sickeningly realize that a muggy, distasteful vent of steam is rising out of the grates that you are standing on in each tower, enveloping you in a faint, damp misery. The impact is real and the artistic evocation of the death camps is nearly overwhelming. The New England Holocaust Memorial turns a visit to a monument into an unforgettable experience.

Over the past quarter century or so, I have visited Europe several times. Now *there* is a place that really knows how to memorialize! Huge Roman monuments, sleek Grecian statues, or centuries-old French memorials seem to appear at every corner in Europe. And while it is the soaring tributes in marble and stone that we read about in history books and see in movies and in travel magazines, there are some quiet and simple memorials that are equally compelling, if not more so. Take World War II, for instance.

Perhaps no other event in world history has as many statues, monuments, and memorials dedicated to it. Virtually every country, *every town* in Europe has a village square or public garden with a monument to the great conflict that enveloped the continent some seven decades ago.

So which is the most fitting?

Maybe it is the hulkingly graceful five-pointed star on the battlefield of Bastogne, in Belgium, where the tide was turned in the Battle of the Bulge, and where US General McAuliffe gave his famous one-word answer to the surrender demands of the Germans (that word was "Nuts!"). The three-stories tall memorial rises out of the dense Ardennes Forest and is inscribed with the names of all the US states and the names of the American units who fought and died there. From the top, it offers a remarkable vista of the now-serene landscape. The horrible carnage of the last-ditch effort by the Germans to win the war there is now peacefully hidden in the dark fir forests that ring the region.

I have been to almost every country in Europe and viewed dozens of magnificent tributes in stone and marble to the events of World War II. But for me, the one monument that really had the greatest impact is just a small outcropping of stones on a rural farm wall on the outskirts of Malmedy, Belgium.

It was a bright August day in 2007 when I arrived there in search of a monument to an event that has captivated me for years. The flowers were in bloom and the sky was as blue as the famous Delft chinaware pattern of nearby Holland.

On December 17, 1944, just outside of the town of Malmedy at what is known as the Baugnez Crossroads, a German battalion came upon an American convoy, which they proceeded to halt by attacking the first and last vehicles in the US column. The Germans, after a brief firefight, captured the remaining GIs and marched them onto a frozen rural Belgium field. And there the American soldiers were machine-gunned in cold blood by their captors, leaving the field soaked with blood. The bodies were left to freeze and were eventually covered by a heavy snowfall. Days later the American forces came to this forsaken place, guided by the few survivors who escaped by running into the woods or by playing dead. The survivors directed their comrades to where the bodies had fallen and they were uncovered. (One of the Malmedy Massacre survivors is the award-winning actor Charles Durning.) The Americans were enraged and a mighty retribution against the Nazis was eventually meted out, both on the battlefield and in the military tribunals after the war.

Having read about this massacre for years, I was quite reluctant to come upon the site of it. But there it was now, right in front of me. A low-slung stone wall was adorned with small nameplates for each of the seventy-four soldiers murdered that day. Fresh flowers were arranged at the foot of the wall. Across the road was the barn that the Germans rolled their machine-gun trucks into to hide their intentions. Behind the barn is the actual field where the killings took place. It is an airy and sunlit place of suffocating sadness.

As I walked the wall, reading off the typical American sounding names of the dead soldiers (Pitt, Carson, Miller, McKinney, Phillips, Scott, Oliver, Cohan,

McGee), the senselessness of it all seeped into my very being. War is hell, they say. And hell was here on that bleak, frozen day nearly seventy years ago. At the end of the wall of names is a plaque with a quotation on it. It reads: "'We here highly resolve that these dead shall not have died in vain.' Abraham Lincoln."

I found the words of Lincoln's address comforting, knowing that the memory of these American boys, so many thousands of miles from home, was being sheltered here in this lonely corner of Belgium, by the words of the Great Emancipator.

To me, this simple stone wall in Malmedy is the greatest, most powerfully eloquent of all the World War II memorials in Europe.

Another find during my globetrotting days is the fierce and patriotic statue of Sir William Wallace (he of "*Braveheart*" fame) tucked away in the woods in the Scottish Borders. I found it while I was on an afternoon trek with my Scottish friend Cameron Oliver and some of his Hawickies named Gus, Ian, Kim, and Drew. We parked on a dirt road just a couple of miles up from the famous Dryburgh Abbey (site of the grave of Sir Walter Scott), opened up a farmer's cow gate, and walked a muddy path about two hundred yards into the woods. The statue, made out of red sandstone and erected in 1813 by the eleventhth Earl of Buchan, soars more than thirty feet into the Scottish sky and captures the Saltaire sentimentalism of this much fought over region perfectly. The nobility of the statue, which is resplendent with crown, shield, and sword, is quite unforgettable. The view from here (known locally as Wallace View) over the checkerboard farm fields of the Tweed Valley is one of the best in Scotland.

From around the world and from sea to shining sea, as I have journeyed I have always hungered for the majesty and historic symbolism of monuments to iconic people and happenings. Having been a resident of Upstate New York for almost my entire life (not withstanding timeouts in the above-mentioned New York City, Los Angeles, and Houston), I have carried on my longtime love affair with my home region and with the monuments that abound. I decided that a travelogue of sorts to the famous and unknown tributes in stone to the great happenings unique to Upstate New York would make an interesting and informative compilation. This book is the result of that research.

I have covered more than two thousand miles of roads to research *Monumental New York!* The selection of monuments included in this book represents a cross section of the many varieties found positioned in our village greens, cemeteries, and courthouse squares. Some pay tribute to towering figures (Franklin and

Eleanor Roosevelt), historic world events (the Irish Famine), historic New York State events (the construction of the Erie Canal), and even curious, whimsical footnotes in history (see the chapter on the statue to Mr. Lincoln's Whiskers). Big cities are represented here (Albany's Firefighters Memorial), as are mid-sized cites (Ithaca's Carl Sagan monument) and even out of the way towns (Saranac Lake's Dr. Trudeau memorial). The subjects of the thirty entries are many, not wanting to dwell heavy-handed on war monuments or solid, sour visages of forgotten or unknown civic leaders. Some are fun (see Rochester's Let's Have Tea monument), some ancient (Geneva's Torture Tree), and some are brand new (Kinderhook's new tribute to its favorite son, President Martin Van Buren). All are fascinating and all have an important story to tell.

The boundaries for the inclusion in *Monumental New York!* are the region around the Tappan Zee Bridge (south), the New England border with New York (east), the St. Lawrence River (north), and Western New York.

For the historic sweep and scope of these unique statues, monuments, and memorials, there is no boundary. Remembered in stone are three US presidents, several battles, a young girl, a heroic dog, a famous prison riot, a special group of American mothers, a French explorer, and many others.

The thirty entries are a mere sampling of the wondrous tributes found in the public realm in virtually every community across Upstate New York. These are some of my favorites, and I hope they will become your favorites too.

So I invite you to come along with me and meet my friends in stone and bronze: the female Paul Revere, the people's astronomer, the white woman of the Genesee, the Sandlot Kid, the *real* Uncle Sam, the men who dug Clinton's Ditch, and many more as we travel together the highways and back roads of the Catskill Mountains, the Leatherstocking Region, Western New York, the Adirondacks, the Hudson Valley, the Capital District, and more, all of them in my own backyard, in beautiful and historic Upstate New York.

Oh, and as for my first statue, monument, or memorial, in my first city? Rest assured that Moses on the Rockpile is the first entry in this book.

PS: My wife, Trish, has been invaluable to me in writing this book. She is an excellent traveling companion, works the map room in the car with great aplomb, and is always interested in our new finds. She is an extremely pleasant woman to accompany me on my far-flung journeys. Trish is enchanted by monuments of all sizes and shapes too. Her favorite is the unforgettable Rodin masterpiece, the Burghers of Calais. French law would allow no more than twelve castings of this giant, immortal work after Rodin died. So far Trish has taken me to visit our friends the burghers at the Rodin Museum in Paris, the House of Parliament in London, the Hirschhorn Museum in Washington, DC, the Met in New York, the Rodin Museum in Philadelphia, and the statue's original casting in the town square (since 1880) in Calais, France. I am sure she has the next stop on our Rodin Tour already mapped out. I must say that without Trish next to me, the research and travels for this book would have been a lot less fun, and the writing of it would have been impossible. Thanks, honey!

Statues, Monuments, and Memorials of Upstate New York

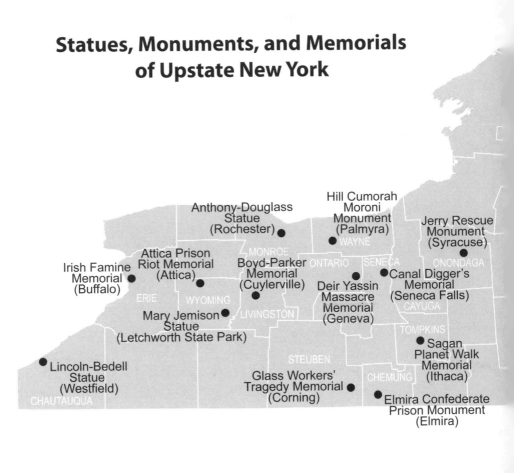

Anthony-Douglass Statue (Rochester)

Hill Cumorah Moroni Monument (Palmyra)

Jerry Rescue Monument (Syracuse)

WAYNE

MONROE ONTARIO SENECA ONONDAGA

Attica Prison Riot Memorial (Attica)

Irish Famine Memorial (Buffalo)

Boyd-Parker Memorial (Cuylerville)

Canal Digger's Memorial (Seneca Falls)

Deir Yassin Massacre Memorial (Geneva)

ERIE WYOMING LIVINGSTON CAYUGA

Mary Jemison Statue (Letchworth State Park)

TOMPKINS

Sagan Planet Walk Memorial (Ithaca)

STEUBEN

Lincoln-Bedell Statue (Westfield)

Glass Workers' Tragedy Memorial (Corning)

CHEMUNG

Elmira Confederate Prison Monument (Elmira)

CHAUTAUQUA

N

0   50
Miles

Syracuse University Cartographic Laboratory

Dr. Trudeau Memorial (Saranac Lake)

John Brown Statue (Lake Placid)

Crown Point Lighthouse (Crown Point)

Knox Cannon Trail Monuments (Fort Ticonderoga and various places)

FRANKLIN

ESSEX

ONEIDA

HERKIMER

Proctor Eagle Monument (Utica)

General Herkimer Monument (Herkimer)

Seabiscuit Statue (Saratoga Springs)

SARATOGA

Sandlot Kid Statue (Cooperstown)

Rufus King Memorial (Albany)

Uncle Sam Memorial (Troy)

OTSEGO

ALBANY

RENSSELAER

SUNY Oneonta 9/11 Memorial (Oneonta)

Van Buren Statue (Kinderhook)

COLUMBIA

Woodstock Concert Monument (Bethel)

Meet the Roosevelts (Hyde Park)

ULSTER

DUTCHESS

McKinley Statue (Walden)

Gold Star Mother Memorial (Kent)

Sybil Ludington Statue (Carmel)

ORANGE

PUTNAM

WESTCHESTER

War Dog Memorial (Hartsdale)

Monumental
NEW YORK!

1

MOSES ON THE ROCKPILE

The Rufus King Memorial, Albany

THE PLACE

Albany, New York, reigns as a regal capital city near the junction of the Mohawk and Hudson Rivers in northeastern New York State. It received its charter in 1686 and is one of the oldest major cities in America. The influences of the town's Old Dutch heritage can be seen in the nuances and flourishes of the storefronts, institutions, and the New York State Capitol. Situated along one of the narrowest parts of the Hudson River, Albany's past *and* future are forever wedded to this waterway, known as America's Rhine.

The massive, ornate Capitol Building, completed in 1899, features hallmarks of both the Romanesque and Renaissance styles. It is one of only a handful of undomed US capitols. It cost $25 million dollars to build, making it at the time the most expensive government building in the country.

Albany, a city of fewer than 100,000 people, is a crazy quilt of disparate neighborhoods that seem to thrive on their diversity. From millionaire townhouses, to impoverished row houses, and from quaint leafy neighborhoods to sky-rise condominiums, Albany is nothing if not different. Threadbare brownstones sit in the shadow of the magnificent Governor's Mansion, and privately owned condos shoulder up against 1950s-style public housing projects in the Historic Pastures area, Albany's first neighborhood. Early Albany settlers, including farmer and war hero Gen. Philip Schuyler, used this area as a communal grazing pasture.

The Empire Plaza (formally designated as the Governor Nelson A. Rockefeller Empire State Plaza) is a sprawling one-hundred-acre multibuilding complex of state government office space and open public areas. One of its buildings, the Corning Tower, soars forty-two stories high, making it the tallest building in the

state outside of New York City. It is named for the former Albany mayor Erastus Corning, who was the longest serving US mayor in history when he died in 1983 during his eleventh four-year term of office.

The building of the plaza in the late 1960s was controversial from the get-go; critics dubbed it Rocky's Edifice Complex. Thousands of people were moved out of this once-thriving, working-class area when construction crews began the demolition of an entire chapter of Albany's past. Where once multigenerational families of immigrants (mostly Italian) worked, learned, and worshiped together, now a struggling landscape of deserted churches, itinerate neighborhoods, and low-income housing exists. After the more than 13,000 white-collar state government employees who work in this area end their day, for the most part, they do not return until the next workday.

Still, hope is alive in this area of Albany. Private home ownership is on the rise, and plans for a massive revitalization project are moving along briskly. Millions of dollars have been spent making the historic Hudson River waterfront

family friendly, and a new mega-million dollar convention center is about to be
built in the heart of downtown.

Albany has beautiful green spaces throughout, including the world-class
Washington Park, designed by Frederick Law Olmsted, architect of New York
City's Central Park. Tulips abound by the thousands in springtime, and the Tulip
Festival held in the park is one of Albany's major celebrations of its Dutch her-
itage. The Albany area is a major northeastern academic hub, and impressive
colleges calling it home include SUNY Albany, College of Saint Rose, Siena,
Albany Law School, Albany Medical College, Albany College of Pharmacy, and
many others.

Albany cannot be accused of not changing with the times. On a new horizon
for a better day for Albany, and many in the Capital Region, is the emergence of
Tech Valley. A concentrated area of research and development in the high-tech
world of computer technology, Tech Valley took great strides toward reality when
IBM announced plans in 2002 to build a new $2.5 billion dollar facility nearby,
and in 2006 AMD trumped it by announcing plans to construct a mammoth $3.2
billion dollar chip facility right outside of Albany.

Henry Hudson would be so proud!

THE MEMORIAL

In the middle of Washington Park, truly one of America's great urban green
spaces, is a breathtaking family tribute in the shape of a historic statue. Officially
called the King Fountain, this statue/monument was constructed in 1893 and was
donated to Washington Park by the family of local financier and politician Rufus
King. The architect was prolific Scottish sculptor J. Massey Rhind. The statue is
incredible.

The image of Moses smiting the stone of Horeb to bring forth water for his
followers is jaw dropping. The biblical figure soars atop a mountain of indigenous
New York State stone, the boulders having been shouldered up the Hudson River
Valley from Storm King Mountain near West Point. The other four hollow-cast
statues scattered over the boulders are life-size human figures representing the
four stages of life: a mother tenderly caring for her two young children represents
Infancy, an adult male with a sword represents Manhood, a comely maiden with
a water urn represents Youth, and an elderly man leaning on his staff represents

Old Age. With Moses's outstretched arms reaching fifteen feet above the ground and with the sheer tonnage of the boulders forming the massive base of the monument, the heft of the King Fountain itself makes its construction even more remarkable.

The statue, known informally by all as the Moses statue, was cleverly constructed with hidden tunnels underneath, allowing access to mechanics when doing repairs to the intricate fountain system within. Water seemingly flows "miraculously" throughout the statue. A giant plaque directly in front of the monument detailing its dedication masks a double-hinged entryway to the roomy underpinnings of the fountain. In the springtime, with thousands of gaily tipped tulips dancing in the breeze around it, the King Fountain is an unforgettable family tribute and public monument.

When brothers Henry and J. Howard King donated this memorial in tribute to their father in 1893, they also established a trust fund valued at more than $3.5 million for perpetual upkeep of the memorial. Albany's Key Bank is currently the lone trustee of this fund.

WHILE HERE

Albany is alive with sites for the visitor to explore, both historic and contemporary. From tours of the state capitol building to tours of the New York State Museum, there is literally something for all ages to enjoy in this famous city. Of special note, a tour of the USS *Slater*, dockside in downtown Albany on the Hudson River, is a highly unusual and fascinating event. Out of the 563 destroyer escorts in the US navy during World War II, the *Slater* is the only one still afloat. It is open to the public, and tours and talks are hosted by navy veterans of varying ages (http://www.ussslater.org).

The city of Albany is dotted with numerous statues and monuments to men, women, places, and events. An unusually kinetic statue of Dr. Martin Luther King Jr. stands fittingly in the city's Lincoln Park. Generals on horseback parade across the region in statuesque tribute to wars fought over several centuries. Public buildings, some among the oldest in the nation, reflect the changing currents of architecture styles down through the years. But for a sheer variety of classic public monument styles, one need not leave the friendly confines of the aforementioned Washington Park.

At the entrance to the park, at Willett Street, is a magnificent bronze bust to Private Henry Johnson, a black World War I hero who is one of Albany's most storied military heroes. The statue, by Vincent Forte, tells of his achievements (he fought with the famed Harlem Hellcats) and his honors. He received his highest commendations for single-handedly fighting off twenty-one Germans attacking his squad. New York State politicians continually plead his case for a posthumous Congressional Medal of Honor. He is buried in Arlington Cemetery.

Another entrance to the park is adorned with a hulking Soldiers and Sailors War Memorial by famed monument maker Hermon Atkins MacNeil. The James Armsby Memorial in the park pays tribute to the founder of several Albany institutions, including Albany Medial Center Hospital. Its creator, Erastus Dow Palmer, was a local artist who became one of the most important American sculptors of his time. His most famous piece, White Captive, shows a delicate nude woman in an aura of defiance to her Indian captors. When it was first shown to the public in 1859, hundreds of art patrons paid twenty-five cents apiece to view it in a New York gallery, as it rotated slowly on a dramatically backlit pedestal.

Also in Washington Park stands a statue in tribute to Scottish writer Robert Burns, by noted Albany sculptor Charles Calverley. This sixteen-foot-tall bronze seated image has been called by experts "the greatest Robert Burns statue in the world." The base is imported Scottish granite. Calverley was most famous for creating more than 250 busts of famous men, and several are located in the halls of government in Washington, DC.

Oddly, the official name of this historic statue is not, as one might think, the Burns Monument. Instead, it is formally known as the more obscure McPherson Legacy to the City of Albany, New York. In 1888, a poor immigrant house worker named Mary McPherson donated her life savings of $30,000 to the park for the erection of a statue in tribute to her homeland's bard. The Scottish maid attached her name to the monument's title. Albany's St. Andrews Society maintains Burns's statue today, and it is the scene of summertime poetry readings put on by the Poets in the Park organization.

From a Harlem Hellcat to Moses on the Rockpile to Scotland's Peasant Poet and more, Washington Park is an outstanding outdoor arena of art.

There is a week's worth of memorable sculptural and architectural wonders in the Albany area, but three in particular are worthy of a second look. One is the must-see Cathedral of the Immaculate Conception, located between the Empire Plaza and the Governor's Mansion. It was dedicated in 1852. The cathedral's towering twin spires are dramatic exclamation points in the city's skyline. Designed and built by Patrick Charles Keely, the most prolific church architect in America, it is currently undergoing a much-needed, expensive rehabilitation. Still, it is an active parish church, albeit one in an ever-shrinking neighborhood. With so many beautiful old churches in the downtown Albany area sitting empty and abandoned (including another one of Keely's historic gems, St. Joseph's), it is heartwarming to experience the cathedral, both as a historic structure and as a place of worship. One of the largest church buildings in America, the cathedral has been the host to many of the world's luminaries over the years and has been the site of much pomp and circumstance (New York governor Al Smith gave away his daughter in marriage here in 1928).

Keely's supporters, of which there are many, keep a close eye on this, one of the most endangered religious landmarks in the state's capital (http://www .keelysociety.com).

One of Albany's most photographed statues stands proudly at the bottom of the front staircase to the Capitol building. It is a massive, fourteen-foot-tall depiction of Civil War hero General Philip Sheridan (a one-time Albany resident) atop his steed in full military regalia. This is a historic piece of art because two of America's deans of sculpture worked on it. John Quincy Adams Ward (famed for his Wall Street statue of George Washington) started the statue but fell ill before completing it. Daniel Chester French (the Lincoln Memorial) finished it.

And finally, since Albany is a major state capital, it is no surprise that there are a number of monuments and memorials in tribute to every imaginable group. Many, including several war memorials, can be found along the State Street (northern) edge of the Empire Plaza in an area known as Memorial Park. These include the New York State Crime Victims Memorial, which is a large boulder with a plaque on it at the end of two long brick paths inscribed with names of crime victims; the EMS Memorial, which honors emergency medical personnel who have died in the line of duty with a granite memorial depicting the EMS tree of life; the New York State Police Memorial, designed by the daughter of a slain trooper; the New York State Women's Veterans Memorial, featuring a soaring Lady Liberty figure; and the Missing Persons Memorial, called a "remorial" signifying the remembrance of missing loved ones. The memorial is a twenty-foot-tall perpetual flame, symbolically lighting the way home for the missing. Many others are placed in the park, including memorials to the great wars of the past.

One in particular has gained national fame for its stunning lifelike depiction and is one of the most visited memorials in the city. It is the hulking, dramatic New York State Fallen Firefighters Memorial. This memorial is well worth the visit to its Plaza sanctuary, nestled before the extraterrestrial looking performance center known as the Egg. The sculpture, created by artist Robert J. Eccleston, depicts two courageous and exhausted firefighters pulling an injured comrade out of harm's way (the turnout gear suggests they represent the 1960s era). Behind this image is a fifty-four-foot-long marble and granite wall with the names of more than two thousand fallen firefighters (since 1806) engraved on it. The bronze trio of heroes stands more than ten feet tall. Many are moved to tears at its sight.

This capital city takes its public art and public spaces very seriously, and the inquisitive visitor will be richly rewarded for spending time investigating the places described in this chapter as well as other treasures the city has to offer.

For a final, whimsical side trip while viewing the array of wonderful public art in Albany, take a short walk or drive down Broadway (one of Albany's major downtown boulevards) to 991 Broadway. You are now in front of the large Arnoff Moving Company Warehouse Building. Cross the street and look up. *Amazing, isn't it!*

"It" is a giant four-ton, two-story-tall replica of the RCA mascot dog Nipper, his familiar black-and-white face cocked at an angle, listening for his master's voice. This legendary landmark was erected atop the former RCA Building at this location in 1954. Nipper was once the tallest feature in the Albany skyline and was featured in the movie *Ironweed*. Sticking out of his ear is a long pole that once held an airplane warning beacon. It now holds a spotlight so Nipper can be seen for miles in the evening. In February the spotlight shines a red glow over the RCA mascot in support of the American Heart Association.

Albany is a beautiful city filled with great public statues, monuments, and memorials—and four-ton corporate mascots! This great city is definitely worth a visit, especially when the tulips are a'bloomin'!

REFERENCE FILE

For further reading about New York's capital city, *Albany Architecture: A Guide to the City,* edited by Diana S. Waite (Mount Ida Press, 1993), offers several chapters on Albany's varying neighborhoods, including one on Washington Park and its many statues. For Internet information regarding Washington Park history and details, visit www.washingtonparkconservancy.org.

2

"A Time to Die"

The Attica Prison Riot Memorial, Attica

In researching and writing *Monumental New York!* one of the greatest pleasures involved was to travel the Upstate New York region and actually visit and document each of the thirty subjects in the book. It was always an exciting and exhilarating moment to pull off the road after many miles of driving and enter the town or city where the sought-after monument was located. Driving through the historic Four Corners of Herkimer to reach the statue of the city's namesake; climbing the small mountain sandwiched between two cemeteries in Utica to reach the aerie home of the Proctor Eagle; hustling along the buzzing sidewalks of the Ithaca Commons, with its busy bookshops and cafés filled with students and tourists, to finally come upon the "spacey" memorial to Carl Sagan; strolling through the thousands of colorful, fragrant tulips on a brilliant May day to find the Moses Statue in Albany's Washington Park: these were all, like almost every other travel experience reflected in this book, memorable, exciting, and positive moments.

This subject of this chapter was different.

Attica, New York, itself is interchangeable with so many of the other small towns of Upstate New York. A Main Street with small, independently owned shops; a public square with a band gazebo and scattered park benches; colorful banners strung over the entranceway to the town telling of some community event coming up; spiking white church spires reaching to the sky (a hallmark of virtually all Upstate New York communities); and a general atmosphere that reflects more of a time twenty years *before* the current one—all of these attributes can be found in tiny Attica, with its neighborly 2,500 citizens comfortably nestled

9

in far western Wyoming County in Upstate New York. The difference that separates this town from the others in the area is its prison.

Attica. Just the mention of its name sparks a foreboding feeling for so many of a certain generation. It is unfortunate, really, because the town itself is quite lovely.

Attica Correctional Prison was built in the 1930s, and as the newest member of New York's penal institutions, it set out to be a role model for the others. Preceding it were the cold, hard legacies of Sing Sing, Auburn, and others, the classic Big Houses where those who went in never came out. Imprisonment inside was harsh, violent, and brutal. Attica ushered in a new era of "enlightened prisons," employing new techniques of incarceration, educational opportunities for inmates, and a generally lessened environment of inmate abuse than the previous, older, "silent prisons," of the 1800s.

Most of the community of Attica has at least one family member who either works at the prison, will work there someday, or is retired from working there. The prison union pays an unusually high wage for this struggling region of the state, and signs of job-related prosperity are reflected in the homes with big, land-scaped yards and the moderately expensive cars parked in the well-paved drive-ways of these homes.

The palpable sense of dread I felt when reading the sign that says "Welcome to Attica, N.Y." stems directly from the events that began to unfold on September 9, 1971. I was twenty-two years old at the time, and what happened here was the biggest news story of the year in America. I will never forget it.

THE MEMORIAL

By 1971, Attica Prison had dissolved into a tense and dangerous place, for both inmates and guards alike. Yard violence was rampant, racial hatred was mani-fest throughout, and conditions were deplorable. The inmate population was a thousand men *over* the suggested limit of twelve hundred. The staff consisted mainly of white, rural young men guarding a populace of young urban men of color. The weather was unusually steamy for early autumn. Draconian mea-sures had been visited upon the hardened inmates of this, New York's largest maximum-security prison. By this time, prisoners were allowed one pail of water a week to "shower" with, and one roll of toilet paper per inmate per month was the rule.

The Thursday morning of "the incident" began with an unruly roll call of prisoners, which went awry when one prisoner was ordered to stay in his cell (leading the other prisoners in the yard to believe that their comrade was being singled out to be beaten by the guards for an offense). Other inmates began fall-ing out of roll call and went to rescue their fellow inmate. They did so, and when a guard was sent to survey the situation, some inmates beat him. After this, the most drastic action an inmate can undertake in a prison environment, there was no turning back. Armed with pieces of jagged glass, lead pipes, baseball bats, and homemade knives, an ever-growing army of inmates rampaged through Attica, destroying property, setting fires, and taking prisoners.

Forty-two guards and civilian personnel were taken hostage after the first twenty-four hours of the takeover. Those in the yard were emboldened by their new high profile, and a list of demands was issued. What appeared to be a rudi-mentary list of basic demands (better medical care, higher salaries for the prison work done by the inmates, wider freedom of religion, etc.) marked a manifesto that authorities believed they could work with. Except for one. The prisoners wanted blanket amnesty for any and all actions taken by them during the riot. No outside authority would agree to this.

A few hostages were released in dribs and drabs, media outlets were allowed in to document the condition in the yard, and an eerie daily humdrum existence began to settle in. A panel of civilian negotiators joined in the daily efforts to end the rebellion, including activists, politicians, and *New York Times* columnist Tom Wicker, who wrote about his tenure as a riot observer and negotiator in his 1975 best-seller *A Time to Die*.

Outside the prison walls, from his private manse along the Hudson River, Governor Nelson Rockefeller refused the public demand of the prisoners (and civilian negotiators) to come to Attica *personally* in a show of good faith for the prisoner's demands. Corrections boss Russell Oswald, fearing an imminent massacre in the prison yard, prepared, at the governor's direction, an assault on the prison to take it back and end the standoff. The mood was grim. Guards were paraded in front of the media with knives to their throats. Hooded inmates warned of torture, castrations, and mass murder as the scenario began to spiral out of control.

On Monday, September 13, at 9:40 a.m., New York State Police helicopters began dropping tear gas canisters into the main inmate area. An army of rain-coated troopers rushed through the main gate firing a ferocious fuselage of two thousand five hundred bullets within just a couple of minutes. Within ten minutes the onslaught was over, with ghastly results.

Twenty-nine inmates were dead, as were ten hostages (whose lethal wounds were later to be certified to have come from their fellow "rescuing" troopers). Calm was restored to the battered prison, and prisoners were returned to their lockups, but not without a series of incredible reprisals meted upon them by the police. Examples of physical torture, taunting, and dehumanization were recorded by the official commission impaneled a year later to analyze the riot and assess proper blame.

The panel chastised Governor Rockefeller for not going to the prison personally at the time of the riot, stating that "it was highly appropriate that he be at the scene of a critical decision involving significant risk of loss of life."

As prisoner lawsuits against the state dragged on for years (a payout of $8 million was ordered to the inmates by a judge in 2000), reconstruction of the prison was ordered and completed, and many of the major players in the Attica Riot moved on or died.

The lives of the family members of the guards who fell that day must not be, and have not been, forgotten here at Attica. Wives had become widows in a heartbeat, and a dozen children or more had been made fatherless in a single day.

So recognizable from the many newscasts and wire photos of the day, the castle-like fortress of Attica prison is instantly referenced when it emerges from a tree-lined roadway just south of the village of Attica. The front lawn is beautifully landscaped, the gleaming guard turrets evoke a fairy-tale castle atmosphere (from the outside armed guards can still be seen walking the wall of the prison), and the words *Attica Correctional Facility* across the front of the entranceway tower seem oddly familiar even to those who have never visited here before.

Directly in front of the main entrance to the prison is the Attica Prison Memorial garden. An oasis of beautiful plantings surrounds a tall granite marker that reminds the passerby of the sacrifices made on September 13, 1971. The text on the monument reads:

In Memory of the Employees Who Gave Their Lives
In The Riot Of September 9–13, 1971
Man's Inhumanity To Man
Makes Countless Thousands Mourn

Edward T. Cunningham
John J. D'Arcangelo, Jr.
Elmer G. Hardie
Herbert W. Jones, Jr.
Richard J. Lewis
John G. Monteleone
William E. Quinn
Carl W. Vallone
Elon F. Werner
Ronald D. Werner
Harrison W. Whelan

A separate stone marker, in front of the guard's memorial, signifies the solemnity and seriousness accorded this event. Buried in this separate spot is a set of keys. A trio of guards protected these keys during the riot until rioting inmates beat them out of their hands. The keys were ceremoniously buried here on the fifteenth anniversary of the start of the worst prison riot in American history. The stone simply reads:

ATTICA PRISON
1971 Prison Riot Keys
Found in D Yard
September 9, 1986

There is no record of a memorial to the dead prisoners.

Attica can be accessed off the New York State Thruway (Batavia exit, 4B). NYS Rt. 98 South then leads to the village, and the prison is one mile south of the business district on Exchange Street.

WHILE HERE

Attica sits in a rolling plain that spreads from the Finger Lakes region to the western cities of Buffalo and Niagara Falls. When visiting the prison memorial, you will be struck at just how rural this area really is. No major tourist attractions surround Attica, but its real appeal, the small towns and natural beauty, are very much in evidence. A drive in a circle of about twenty-five miles around the village of Attica will take you through pretty communities and bucolic landscapes. A leisurely afternoon drive will take you through one-stoplight towns like Orangeville, Dale, and Varysburg. Two pleasant, lengthier stopovers are beautiful Bennington (named for its larger sister city of Bennington, Vermont) and Warsaw. Warsaw, in particular, boasts many fine Victorian homes and a vividly documented history as an abolition center and Underground Railroad depot in the early 1800s. It was an early, important town in the women's rights movement: Susan B. Anthony gave a key public speech here at the United Church of Warsaw, and the town's library contains an autographed copy of her *History of Woman's Suffrage.*

REFERENCE FILE

The definitive account of the days leading up to, during, and after the prison riot are best chronicled by award-winning *New York Times* reporter Tom Wicker in his 1975 book *A Time to Die: The Attica Prison Revolt* (Crown Publishing). A substantial Internet reference site called Talking History chronicles the riot and its aftermath. It can be found at www.talkinghistory.org/attica.

3

THE TORTURE TREE

The Boyd-Parker Memorial, Cuylerville

THE PLACE

Cuylerville, New York, is a suburb of the college town Geneseo, its neighbor to the immediate east. An area rich with natural beauty, several key tourist components of the upstate region are within just a few short miles from here. Cuylerville, a small hamlet of about 300 residents, played a major role in the development of Western New York in its transformation from a bastion of Indian tradition, culture, and commerce into an empty and inviting frontier for further western settlement by white settlers.

Little Beard's Town was the name of the Seneca Indian "capital," located near today's Cuylerville. Seneca Chief Little Beard (Sword Hanging Down) had been the source of constant irritation to George Washington and his colonists. The chief had sided with Great Britain during the Revolutionary War and had aided the British in their attacks on white settlements throughout Northern New York. He was present at the Cherry Valley Massacre on November 11, 1778. This terrible attack, in which the settlers were murdered and scalped (including thirty women and children), has long been considered the single act that triggered General Washington to send Generals John Sullivan and James Clinton north and west through New York to wage a "scorched earth" assault on the Indian nations of the state to settle what Washington called "the Indian problem." He in fact employed a full quarter of his entire army in the Clinton-Sullivan Campaign.

With Clinton in the east and Sullivan in the New York/Pennsylvania border area, a pincer-like movement began, squeezing the Indians from their homes and resulting in large numbers of killed. More than forty villages were burned to the ground, and crops were destroyed. This military movement basically laid waste

16

to the region and scattered the members of the Seneca Indian Nation (and other tribes) to the winds. It left an empty space where villages once thrived (for more than one hundred years), and the void was quickly filled with white settlers pushing farther west in the state after the war was over.

Of the forty villages wiped out by the expedition, Little Beard's Town was the last and the most western. It was also the scene of an unforgettably horrific act by the desperate Seneca on their flight ahead of the pursuing soldiers. In retaliation to this act, the town was erased from the face of the earth by Generals Sullivan and Clinton. Only one landmark remained where once a bustling and prosperous civilization thrived.

That landmark is the Torture Tree.

THE MEMORIAL

In mid-September 1779, General Sullivan forded the Conesus Lake inlet at present-day Geneseo and mapped an attack on the major Seneca village of Genesee Castle (near present-day Cuylerville). Uncertain exactly where the village was, he ordered Lt. Thomas Boyd and Sgt. Michael Parker to take a small party into the woods on a scouting mission. Accompanied by twenty-eight men, the party was ambushed along the way. Most of the soldiers were killed, and Boyd and Parker were captured. These choice battle prizes were marched to the tribal council where they were interrogated by Mohawk Chief Joseph Brant, Seneca Chief Little Beard, and an American sympathetic to the British, John Butler. Butler and his son, Captain Walter Butler, had been intimately involved with several massacres along the western front (the Wyoming Massacre in Pennsylvania and the Cherry Valley Massacre), and were hated and feared by the Americans.

This council ordered the torture and death of the two American officers. Boyd and Parker were taken to a large oak tree, stripped and tied up. The torture they endured is almost beyond belief. They were whipped bloody, had their toe and fingernails ripped off, and then piece by piece were slowly chopped up (taking great care to keep the soldiers alive as long as possible). After their ears and eyes were removed they were left hanging from the tree trunk by their own intestines for the mercifully short time it took them to finally die. They were then beheaded.

A short time after this orgy of evil took place, Sullivan's army came searching for their missing men. Clearly, the sight they came upon at the Torture Tree was ghastly. Sgt. Parker's head was never found; Boyd's was discovered, skinned and impaled on a spear. General Sullivan ordered the immediate burial of his officers' remains along the creek near the tree. After, he marched on Genesee Castle (also known by the Indian name *Chennusio,* hence the English translation to Geneseo) and ordered its obliteration. The enraged soldiers vented their anguish over the torture deaths of their officers with mighty retribution. The Indian village was virtually eliminated, with every house burned, every field scorched, every animal slaughtered. The Senecas fled in fear and dispersed throughout the countryside.

The destruction of Genesee Castle marked the final violent orgasm of the Clinton-Sullivan Campaign and marked the most western point of their expedition.

Today, on the quiet roadside between present day Geneseo and Cuylerville (Route 39E, two miles west of Geneseo) stands a powerful yet simple tribute to the heroic officers. A huge boulder, standing in front of the Torture Tree, bears a plaque with these words on it:

This wayside shrine marks the place where on September 14, 1779, two young soldiers of the Revolution, Lt. Thomas Boyd and Sgt. Michael Parker, met death undaunted in the line of Duty, after lingering torture they marked with their blood the western limit in the state of NY for the great struggle for American freedom.

This solemn area is today known as the Boyd-Parker Memorial Park and is maintained by the Town of Leicester for public use.

The graves of Boyd and Parker remained in Cuylerville for more than one hundred years, until grave robbers found them and began stripping their bodies of valuable Revolutionary War relics, such as uniform buttons and medals. In August 1882, they were reinterred with great ceremony at Mt. Hope Cemetery in Buffalo, where a plaque at their grave tells of their heroism and tragic deaths.

Note: A New York State Historical marker on the village green in Cuylerville is identical to the one found at Boyd-Parker Memorial Park just outside of town. This village green location is *not* the site of the Torture Tree. At the tree itself, there is a special bronze plaque, authorized by the National Arborists Association, denoting it as "a tree that was in existence during the American Revolution."

WHILE HERE

Cuylerville is on the northern doorstep of Letchworth State Park, the jewel of the New York State Park system and home of the Grand Canyon of the East (see chapter 15 for details of the park). Geneseo, just two miles east of Cuylerville, is worth a quick visit. This was Indian territory in the late 1700s when the Senecas were based here by the hundreds. It was the heart of Seneca commerce, agriculture, and culture. The fertile landscape produced much of what the Indians consumed, and even today the area is considered to be the bread basket of New York.

The college town of Geneseo is well preserved and displays great architectural beauty. Many of the buildings along the movie set–like Main Street have been greatly cared for and reflect the intricate architectural flourishes that hallmark the designation of the entire community as a National Historic Landmark (1991). It is one of only eight cities in the United States so deemed.

The Treaty of Big Tree (Geneseo) was held here in 1794, transferring ownership of hundreds of square miles of land west of the Genesee River. Robert

Morris, the richest man in America and a signer of the Declaration of Independence, sent representatives, and the great Seneca chief and orator Red Jacket spoke for the Indians. A council fire was lit at a site along what is now Main Street, and hundreds of Seneca warriors, chiefs, and their families made their way to the village. The negotiations were difficult for both parties (the Indians had given up much of their land in the previous years, and this was basically their last stand). Morris eventually paid $100,000 for all but three parcels (which remained reservations), and the dominance of the Iroquois Six Nations in Western New York ended.

A famous tavern and inn is located today where the Treaty of Big Tree took place (unfortunately, the famous twenty-seven feet in diameter white birch tree where the treaty was signed was lost in an 1857 flood). The Big Tree Inn, at 46 Main Street, opened its doors on September 13, 1886. It is one of the most historic inns of Western New York. Sitting high atop a ridge, the back of the inn offers a twenty-mile view across the rolling Genesee Valley. Among the many famous guests at the inn over the years have been actress Jean Harlow, author Samuel Clemens (Mark Twain), and President Theodore Roosevelt.

The campus of SUNY Geneseo (the "Harvard of the SUNY System") is worth a walk-through also. Many of the buildings are old and beautiful, and the vistas over the valley are awesome (legend has it that *National Geographic Magazine* once listed the sunset view from the Geneseo Campus Gazebo as one of the ten most beautiful in America). There are five thousand students at SUNY Geneseo, and five thousand residents of the town of Geneseo, making it the classic "town and gown" community.

One thing that both the students and the citizens of Geneseo can truly agree on is the charm of the Bear Fountain on Main Street. This delightful European touch has been a working fountain (first for horses and later for visitors) since the late 1800s. It depicts a playful little bear frolicking in a small pool of water. Villagers dutifully decorate the whimsical fountain for various holidays, and students diligently pour soap bubbles into it as a rite of graduation!

REFERENCE FILE

Many books tell the story of New York State's involvement in the Revolutionary War, including the famous Clinton-Sullivan Campaign. One that is most interesting is *New York State: The Battleground of the Revolutionary War* by Hamilton Fish (Vantage Press, 1976). The author was a former New York State congressman. An exhaustive Web site that highlights the entire war operation of the campaign, including photos and maps, can be found at http://www.sullivan clinton.com.

4

THE GREAT HUNGER

The Irish Famine Memorial, Buffalo

Buffalo is New York State's second largest city, behind New York City. The most recent census puts the total of residents at around 300,000. This is a significant number, but becomes even more significant when you factor in the *quarter of a million residents who have left* Buffalo since the urban decline began along the Rust Belt in the 1950s. The city was built for a greater number of citizens than there are here, and that is a double-edged sword for the Queen City. While the declining public tax base has made budgets tighter and tighter over the years, the city, with tens of thousands of residents drained from it, seems almost dreamlike to a casual visitor.

Like the big city it once was, Buffalo still boasts some of America's most beautiful public parks, a robust waterfront area, first-class medical centers, respected universities, architecture of unparalleled quality, wide boulevards evocative of European cities, and a vibrant social and sports scene. And all this with a couple of hundred thousand residents less than just two generations ago. One is struck by how, well, *roomy* this city really is!

Delaware Avenue is one of the grandest of Upstate New York's Main Streets. Radiating for miles in a straight line from downtown (Buffalo was designed in 1804 as a radial and grid city, one of only three in America), the street is a virtual catalog of major, important residences keynoting Buffalo's glorious past (for example, stop by the amazing French Regency–style mansion at 888 Delaware Avenue, the former home of Charles Goodyear, of tire fame).

In the early to mid-1800s, Buffalo was one of the busiest ports in the nation. Wharfs lined the shoreline of Lake Erie, and boats of all sizes plied their trades

from large warehouses stacked row upon row. Over a dozen large steamboats sailed the Great Lakes, taking nearly fifty thousand itinerants west to Chicago in the 1830s alone. Canal Street, which runs the entire length of the waterfront, was dotted with hundreds of saloons and brothels and garnered the dubious title of the Wickedest Street in World. The city was one of the most active terminals of the Underground Railroad, and "conductors" here guided hundreds of escaped slaves to freedom across Lake Erie to Canada.

Buffalo was the first major city in America to be completely illuminated by the electric light. It is the home of the first nondairy creamery product (Buffalo inventor Robert Rich's topping preceded Cool Whip by twenty-two years!). It was the death place of an American president: President William McKinley was shot at the Buffalo Pan-American Exposition's Temple of Music on September 6, 1901. He died on September 14, 1901, at the Milburn residence at 1168 Delaware Avenue (a marker tells of this address's significance). And, it was the birthplace of one of America's most beloved, original snack items: Buffalo wings. On October

16, 1964, Teressa Belissimo took some soon-to-be-thrown-away chicken wings, deep-fried them up for her son, Dominic, sloshed them through a tub of hot sauce, and voila! Their bar at 1047 Main Street, the Anchor Bar (it is still there) became the home for this Super Bowl (and any other time) craving. It is as close to a New York landmark eatery as it gets.

The docks of the Buffalo waterfront have received many strange cargos over the years, from all four corners of the world. But none were as sad and desperate as the cargo on the ships that clogged the harbor in the mid-nineteenth century. Wave after sorrowful wave of Irish immigrants arrived just a breath ahead of the potato famine that had decimated their homeland. They arrived here from inland, too, by canal boat and train. Nearly one and a half million Irish immigrants came to America at this time, and while many East Coast cities took a large share of these poor souls (Boston and New York in particular), Buffalo took an enormous proportion of Irish as compared to the city's relatively small population. In a five-year period ending around 1850, more than ten thousand Irish immigrants entered Buffalo to seek a better life.

Buffalo would be changed forever.

THE MEMORIAL

In 1849, a blight tore through the landscape of Ireland, wiping out potato fields in every corner of the country. (The potato was the Irish cash crop and dietary mainstay.) People lost their land, homes, and lives on an unparalleled scale. The resulting medical calamity is considered one of the classic natural tragedies of all times. Imprecise as the calculations inherently are, conventional wisdom puts the death toll in the tiny country of Ireland at one million. More than that fled their homeland. Ireland's population went from eight million to six million in one record-keeping period. Conditions were harsh at home. The ruling English government had enacted a brutal taxation and eviction policy against the Irish, and many threw their lot in with chance and luck as they crossed "the bowl of tears" (Atlantic Ocean) in unsafe and overcrowded boats dubbed "coffin ships" and came to America.

Buffalo opened wide its arms to the immigrants. Charity organizations and social service groups cared for the families arriving in wretched condition. Work was found for the men. Housing was provided, mostly along the waterfront area along Lake Erie. The city had already established itself as an Irish-friendly community (Isaac Harrington was elected Buffalo's first Irish mayor in the years just before the famine sent his compatriots to America), and the new citizens were welcome. Many Irish immigrants suffered abuses, violence, and intolerance by Americans in the overcrowded tenements of the East Coast cities, but in the more friendly neighborhoods of inland New York State, these conditions, although present, were not as severe.

At the site of the end of their pitiful journey, the Western New York Irish Famine Memorial now remembers the Irish immigrants who fled *An Gorta Mor,* the Great Hunger. There are many memorials and monuments, mostly in the East, paying homage to this event, and they are always moving and emotional tributes. Three of the most important are in Boston, Philadelphia, and New York City. In Boston, at the corner of School and Washington Streets, a double sculpture depicts the Irish arriving in the city gaunt and skeletal, ragged families whose despair is clearly etched in their faces. The second sculpture shows the same family healthier, happier, and prideful of their newfound home in the States. In New York City, the memorial to the famine immigrants is located near the footprint of the World Trade Center and features a replica of a barren Irish shanty (roofless to evoke the missing inhabitants), and a trailway snakes under and above ground through a typical Irish landscape until the visitor "exits" at a promontory looking out at the Statue of Liberty. In Philadelphia (at Penn's Landing) is a massive depiction of the fleeing Irish families aboard a rickety coffin ship. It includes no less than thirty-five life-sized figures in various states of woe. All three monuments are incredible.

Buffalo's tribute is no less amazing. It is rife with symbolism, and it is all the more moving because it is placed in the exact spot where so many of the ten thousand fleeing Irish first set foot on Buffalo soil. There are no statues, no gaunt faces, and no proclamations. Only stone. The concept is brilliant. As it is told on the accompanying panels at the entranceway to the memorial, the giant granite native Irish stone in the middle is jarringly off center to the memorial site, symbolic of the scattering of the populace during the famine years, the Irish Diaspora. Thirty-two jagged boulders ring the center stone, each one representing a county in Ireland. Movingly, these stones, donated by the citizens of Cork, Ireland, were actual stones dismantled from the dock in Ireland from which many of the immigrants embarked to reach America. An empty well represents the Great Silence, a period when no one would speak of the horrors of the event they lived through. A Gaelic saying is chiseled among the stones in the courtyard: "If these were to be silent, the very stones would cry out."

Again, the location of this memorial, right on the waterfront with the city skyline behind it, makes it so poignant and so powerful. To quote directly from the memorial plaque: "The Western New York Irish Famine Memorial is within view of the old Erie Canal, the grain and steel mills, and other industry that flourished with Irish labor. It is here that the Irish lived, worked and secured liberty for themselves and their families."

Monumental New York! is written as a historical guidebook to the places that pay tribute to important dates and people in our history, in the Upstate New York region. Some of the entries in the book are place specific (Attica Prison, the Sandlot Kid). Others remind us of events that touched all Americans and, therefore, are memorialized in dozens of places (September 11, for example). Such is the case with the Irish famine tragedy, and although there are numerous places to observe memorials to this event and the people who braved it, I believe that the Western New York Irish Famine Memorial in Buffalo is among the simplest and yet most potent tributes of them all.

WHILE HERE

Much could be packed into a long weekend in Buffalo, but if I were to offer a Top Five list of my own favorites I would include one of the great museums in the city (there are many), the Albright-Knox Gallery, 1285 Elmwood Avenue. It is a bountiful harvest of Picassos, Pollocks, Warhols, and van Goghs. For a surprise that will stay with you for a long time, gape in awe at *The Horse Fair*, by one of the most preeminent (yet rarely seen) female masters, Rosa Bonheur. It is breathtaking. Next I would visit the site of President McKinley's death and Teddy Roosevelt's swearing in, which is now operated by the National Parks Service. The Milburn Home is at 1168 Delaware Avenue, and it is one of only a few swearing-in presidential sites not in Washington, DC. Follow this up with a trip out to 1411 Delaware Avenue to Forest Lawn Cemetery (one of Upstate New York's premier burial grounds). Guided or self-guided tours will take you to the final resting places of President Millard Fillmore, Seneca Chief Red Jacket, inventor Willis

Carrier (air conditioning), Sara Hinson (founder of Flag Day), funk-master and Grammy Award winner Rick James, and many more.

Next, take a tour of the unbelievable architecture represented in Buffalo. It is mind-boggling: Frank Lloyd Wright has houses here; Frederick Law Olmsted, of New York City's Central Park fame, has parks here; I. M. Pei has facades here; Stanford White has buildings here; the American Arts and Craft Movement began here; and on and on it goes.

And last but not least wrap up your day with a steaming plate of Anchor Bar Buffalo wings. They are spicy, sloppy, and perfect in every way!

As a bonus for all you military fans out there, the USS *Little Rock,* a famous US Navy battleship, is permanently docked near the famine memorial. The ship is open to the public.

REFERENCE FILE

There is no shortage of books about Buffalo. With its great sports teams, parks, and great museums (and hot wings!), there is a book about almost everything. For a comprehensive book for the visitor heading to Buffalo, the official visitor guide (free and available online from the city's tourist and convention organization at http://www.visitbuffaloniagara.com) is useful and filled with great city information.

The city's legendary Anchor Bar has a great Web site, too, and you can order some of their famous hot wing sauce at http://www.anchorbar.com.

THE BUILDERS OF CLINTON'S DITCH

The Canal Digger's Memorial, Seneca Falls

Few of the smaller communities in Upstate New York have as rich a palette of assets as does centrally located Seneca Falls. With a population of just 7000, a picture-book downtown area dripping with nostalgia, side streets dotted with grand Victorian painted ladies, historic landmarks at every corner, and a "river running through it" (well, the serene Seneca River and later, the human-made Cayuga-Seneca Canal), one has the urge to tag the village as "perfect." Deniers would be hard-pressed to convince otherwise.

Once the domain of the Cayuga Indian tribe, the village (and much of the surrounding area) was decimated by the forces of Generals Clinton and Sullivan during the Clinton-Sullivan Campaign of 1779. After the hostilities, the land around Seneca Lake was set aside for veterans of the army and was settled by them.

The natural series of waterfalls along the river was the fount from which much of the success of Seneca Falls sprang. Mills producing everything from distilled alcohol to lumber thrived along the waterway, and in the mid-1800s Seneca Falls was the third largest flour producer *in the world!* The rotary water pump was invented here by Birdsall Holly Jr., and, after he partnered with industrialist Seabury Gould, their company, Goulds Pumps, became one of the largest pump makers in the nation. The company still has a manufacturing base in the community.

The Cayuga-Seneca Canal was completed in 1915, basically transforming the lazy Seneca River into a watercraft highway connecting two of New York's Finger Lakes, Seneca Lake and Cayuga Lake. Today, pleasure craft of all sizes

and types leisurely glide through town, offering up an unusual and fun twist to people watching. The Cayuga-Seneca Canal is now a part of the New York State Canal System.

Seneca Falls is the birthplace of the women's rights movement. Thousands of visitors from all over America (and the world) make the pilgrimage to the village each year to pay tribute to the five courageous women and their band of followers who in 1848 daringly held a convention here dedicated to a reformation of the role women played in the homes, workplaces, schools, *and* ballot boxes of the nation. The saga of the movement and these five female pioneers (Elizabeth Cady Stanton, Lucretia Mott, Martha Wright, Mary Ann M'Clintock, and Jane Hunt) is well documented throughout the community in displays, historic homes (many open to the public), monuments, museums, and public dedications. Susan B. Anthony would join the women's rights movement later in 1851.

With the possible exception of Cooperstown, no other small village in Upstate New York offers more for the visitor in history, beauty, *and* importance than does "the central gateway to the historic Finger Lakes," Seneca Falls.

THE MEMORIAL

Although the "Cay-Sen" Canal runs only about a dozen miles, connecting two of the nearest Finger Lakes, its concept, construction, and ultimate use is a reflection of the New York canal system as a whole. The state features almost three hundred miles of canals, and the official Canalway Trail system takes you over 260 miles of waterways, including the Erie Canal. Much of the nearly two-century-old canal system is still in evidence along the trail today, and many of the towns that still have old canal sites and locks highlight them as part of their community's historic significance. It is hard to imagine the explosive growth of New York City as the world's greatest port without taking a look at its back door waterway from the nation's interior along the Erie Canal. Governor DeWitt Clinton (the subject of the mocking sobriquet of Clinton's Ditch) drove the idea of a statewide interconnecting waterway for years and recognized the incredible construction hazards entailed in its completion. The resulting canalway construction was considered to be an engineering marvel of the age.

Tens of thousands of immigrants flooded into Upstate New York to toil in the unsafe conditions of 1800s canal work. The overwhelmingly Yankee workforce was augmented by a large contingent of Irish immigrants in the building of the original Erie Canal in 1825. It is said that the Irish did their backbreaking work for a half-dollar and a jigger of whiskey a day, and the Italians, who came nearly a century later to build the Barge Canal, would enjoy their short nights attending the three-penny operas at opera houses that sprang up along the canal route for that very purpose (some of these early theaters are still standing in Upstate New York). German and Welsh immigrant miners would later contribute by mining the native limestone used for the locks. The mortality rate, from accidents as well as disease, was high.

One of the most deadly areas of construction was the Montezuma Marsh, five miles east of Seneca Falls. Here in a teeming, festering backwater swamp, more than one thousand Irish and American canal workers died of malaria in summer of 1819. The death toll was so astronomical that construction of the entire project was halted until winter (when the disease-bearing mosquitoes would be gone). However, the winter of 1819–20 turned out to be brutal, and many additional immigrant canal workers died of frostbite.

Along the canal in the downtown area of Seneca Falls (on the southern bank) is an unusual and fitting tribute to the Italian and Irish canal workers who gave their all to the completion of their task. The Frank Ludovico Sculpture Trail is an odd conglomeration of Seneca Falls tributes in bronze, metal, and stone. The trail, a meandering dirt path that follows the canal, connects two of the village's bridges and offers a beautiful view of the downtown area and the waterway with its boats and docks. Among the sculptures are tributes to the women's rights movement; a bust of a Native American woman; a life-size bronze statue of Amelia Bloomer, a women's rights activist and creator of the then shocking bloomer pants; a tribute to Christian Science founder Mary Baker Eddy; and some modern art sculptures and attractive landscaping. All in all, the quiet river setting makes a peaceful and relaxing background for a walk (in all seasons) along this unique art trail.

On August 7, 2005, the newest additions to the Ludovico gallery were dedicated. They are unusual and quite moving. Two life-size statues, one of an Italian canal worker, the other an Irish worker, stand *in the canal* as if caught in the act of their typical construction day. Walking along the tree-shrouded trail, one is taken aback upon coming upon these two figures, which, initially, you almost expect to look up and speak to you. Each worker holds the tools of his trade and is amazingly lifelike.

Brian Pfeiffer, of Bennington, New York, created these concrete sculptures, each of which weighs a ton. His technique, unusual for sculptors, is to pour concrete over an infrastructure of metal rebar and wire mesh forms. A flight of wooden steps allows the visitor to go right down to the water's edge and view the sculptures up close.

To reach the Ludovico Sculpture Trail, go over the Bridge Street bridge at Fall Street (in the downtown area). Park immediately at the end of the bridge, and the trail is along the southern bank. Signs point the way.

The site was formerly a Lehigh Valley Railroad track bed.

WHILE HERE

The Women's Rights National Historical Park encompasses many of Seneca Falls' most important venues. The homes of many of the original central figures of this historic chapter in American history are open to the public for tours and are magnificent. The National Women's Rights Museum is a modern, state-of-the-art multistory building filled with displays, artifacts, video presentations, and photographs. A gift shop stocked with interesting souvenirs is in the front of the building.

Next door to the museum is the heartbeat of the village, the Wesleyan Chapel. It is an astounding example of historic preservation, even though the building was almost completely gone by the time the preservationists got to it in 1985. The chapel was built in 1843, and five years later it was the site of the first women's rights convention. Just a few walls and some roof beams remain of the original Wesleyan Chapel, but what is left is well preserved. As you walk among the remaining remnants, you will view the rolling hillside where the three hundred conventioneers (some two hundred sixty brave women and forty men) sat in wooden pews in 1848. Tranquil flowing waters pour over the chiseled words of the women's Declaration of Sentiments. Many will find the experience transfixing and inspirational. This is clearly one of America's great historical treasures.

Interestingly, of the throng of women who attended the 1848 convention in Seneca Falls, only sixty-eight signed the historic Declaration of Sentiments. Of those sixty-eight, only one, Charlotte Woodward, a nineteen-year-old glove stitcher, was still alive in 1920 to see the law enacted that allowed her to legally cast a vote. She then was then ninety years old.

The National Women's Hall of Fame (at 76 Fall Street, which is basically Seneca Falls' Main Street) is a much-visited repository of tributes and memorabilia of its many inductees. Well over two hundred women have been enshrined in the Hall as of this writing. Among the recent inductees are chef Julia Child, original women's rights conventioneer Martha Coffin Wright, and Henrietta Szold, founder of the Jewish women's organization Hadassah.

Most of the central tourist destinations regarding Seneca Falls' connection to the women's rights movement are within a short walking distance in the small downtown area of the village.

While here, go just north of the Bridge Street bridge to view an amazing piece of outdoor sculpture. Alongside of the river road, with the quaint village as a backdrop, is a life-size triple sculpture that is one of the most photographed sights in Seneca Falls. The three five-foot-tall bronze statues represent Amelia Bloomer (in her bloomers) introducing Susan B. Anthony to Elizabeth Cady

Stanton. The artist is A. E. Ted Aub, and the sculpture was given to the village of Seneca Falls by New York Governor George Pataki on July 18, 1998. The title is *When Anthony Met Stanton*, and it recreates the actual chance meeting on the streets of Seneca Falls of these three female pioneers in May 1851.

By the way, the Bridge Street Bridge is quite famous itself. Well-known local lore recalls that movie director Frank Capra was a visitor to Seneca Falls in the early 1940s, a period in which he was writing the screenplay for his new movie. He was captivated by the small town qualities of the community and is said to have incorporated many of its places and people into the film. The movie was the classic *It's a Wonderful Life,* and the Bridge Street bridge is the model for the bridge that Jimmy Stewart's character jumps off at the beginning of the film. A plaque on the bridge today tells this amusing anecdote, and if you look up you will see that the entrance roads to the bridge structure are marked with signs reading "George Bailey Lane" and "Bedford Falls Avenue." You exit the bridge at "Angel Avenue" and "Clarence Street."

An old downtown landmark has recently undergone a multi-million-dollar renovation in hopes of it acting as a catalyst for a surge in movie buffs visiting here. The brand new Hotel Clarence (http://www.hotelclarence.com) opened in 2009 at 108 Fall Street and carries the theme of the beloved movie *It's a Wonderful Life* throughout its many rooms.

REFERENCE FILE

An excellent book on the history of Seneca Falls is *All Men and All Women Are Created Equal: The Story of the Women's Rights National Historical Park* by Joanne M. Hanley (Eastern National Publishing Co., 1997). For Internet information regarding the entire Finger Lakes region, with a highlight on Seneca Falls and its many historic sites, go to http://www.lifeinthefingerlakes.com.

The Canal Workers sculptor, Brian Pfeiffer, also has a Web site that features a listing and photos of his public commissions at http://www.asculptorsoul.com.

PLAY BALL!

The Sandlot Kid Statue, Cooperstown

Cooperstown, New York, is as American as Kate Smith, apple pie, and . . . baseball!

In the geographic center of New York State, Cooperstown is a village seemingly impervious to economic downturns. It welcomes more than a quarter million visitors *every* year, regardless of depressions, recessions, wars, and sky-high gas prices. Since 1939, when the doors of the National Baseball Hall of Fame first swung open on one-stoplight Main Street, generations of families have traveled the serpentine, well-beaten paths to this small town, first in their small-windowed black sedans, then in wooden-paneled, multihued station wagons, and now in sleek hybrids, SUVs, and minivans. It is, however, important to remember that even before 1939, Cooperstown was a cultural, literary, and historic landmark of national proportions.

Situated on the southern shore of author James Fenimore Cooper's beloved Glimmerglass (correctly known as Lake Otsego), the village (never more than 2,000 permanent residents) has that magical combination of breathtaking natural beauty, loads of history, and tons of money! Huge family fortunes have been lavished upon the grounds, homes, and facilities of Cooperstown over the years, from the members of the Cooper family themselves, to the philanthropic Clark family (keepers of the Singer sewing machine millions), to the beer-making Busch family as well as to a blue book full of other less well-known and smaller Fort Knoxes.

The village boasts perhaps the finest hospital in rural America, the Mary Imogene Bassett Hospital; the headquarters of the New York State Historical Association, on the site of James Fenimore Cooper's early nineteenth-century farmhouse; the wondrous Farmers' Museum, with its famous folk legend, the Cardiff Giant; the Glimmerglass Opera, which, when it opened in June 1987, was

the first new opera house built in America in more than twenty years; one of the premier grand hotels of New York State, the century-old Otesaga Resort Hotel; and more. And all of this situated on a pastoral, pristine nine-mile lake that gives birth to the mighty Susquehanna River.

"The Village of Museums," located in an area referred to by locals as Leatherstocking Country, is seventeen miles north of I-88, at the Oneonta exit. The interstate travels across the midsection of the state from Binghamton to Albany. The entire village is one of the most popular tourist destinations of the Empire State in all four seasons and offers, at the very least, a busy weekend's worth of history, art, great food, and baseball!

THE STATUE

The Sandlot Kid stands in front of Doubleday Field, the "birthplace of baseball," on Main Street. The statue shows a young farm boy, presumably (from his dress) playing a pickup game of baseball with his friends in a rural setting. Barefoot and wearing overalls and a straw hat, bat perched on his shoulder, the future Hall of Famer stares down the opposing pitcher and dreams of scoring the winning run. The bronze statue stands about twelve feet tall and is without a doubt the most popular photo opportunity in all of Cooperstown.

The Sandlot Kid was created by Italian American sculptor Victor Salvatore (1885–1965). His works have been exhibited at many major museums including the Whitney Museum of American Art, the Metropolitan Museum of Art, the Art Institute of Chicago, and others. His specialty was figurine sculpture, and he studied with the great Gutzon Borglum, who created Mount Rushmore.

An interesting footnote to the story of Victor Salvatore is that he was married to Ellen Ryerson, the "daughter who stayed home." Her father, wealthy industrialist Arthur Ryerson, along with her mother and three siblings, were aboard the HMS *Titanic* when it went down in the Atlantic Ocean on the night of April 14, 1912. Her mother, two sisters, and a brother were saved. Her father went down with the ship and perished.

There are a series of notable, popular sculptures and memorials in this small village. A short walk from Main Street down to the water's edge will bring you to the Indian Hunter by John Quincy Adams Ward (1830–1910) at Lakefront Park. It depicts an Indian scout, bow at ready, and his trusty dog stealthily on the lookout for the unknown ahead. Hailed as the greatest success of the 1867 Paris Exposition, there are four copies of this American icon. The original is in Central Park, New York City, where on February 4, 1869, the Indian Hunter was chosen to be the first statue to be positioned in the park. Other castings are in Cooperstown and Buffalo (Delaware Park), and there is one over the sculptor's grave in Urbana, Ohio.

Back up just above Main Street one will find a striking series of baseball-themed images in the sculpture park between the Baseball Hall of Fame and its research library. Here you will see a life-sized statue of a Dorothy "Mickey" Maguire playing baseball (representing the barnstorming women's leagues of the forties and fifties), a statue of the great pitcher Satchel Paige in full stretch (representing the Negro League players), and a remarkable depiction of the 1955 World Series between the New York Yankees and the Brooklyn Dodgers. This sculpture shows Dodger ace Johnny Podres throwing to catcher Roy Campanella in the final inning of the game. This exciting statue is built to the exact specifications of a major league baseball diamond (distance between the pitcher's mound and home plate, the height of the mound, etc.). It is an emotional favorite of the thousands who view it each year, especially those who hold near and dear the memories of Ebbetts Field and Dem Bums. All three were executed by American sculptor Stanley Bleifeld. More baseball depictions are planned for this area.

Perhaps the most famous statue in Cooperstown is an homage to James Fenimore Cooper himself. Unveiled on August 31, 1941, at the end of the 150th-anniversary celebration of Cooper's arrival in the village as an infant, a giant "seated Cooper" towers over the landscape in a massive, serene evocation of the thoughtful, contemplative author. Holding his top hat and walking stick, the cross-legged colossus gazes out over Lake Otsego from Cooper Park, the exact site of his family's first home, Otsego Hall, which burned down in 1852. Cooper Park itself is now incorporated into the Baseball Hall of Fame campus.

Cooperstown also is the home to an amazing World War I memorial. This tribute to the "Doughboy" stands at the intersection of Lake and Pine Streets, directly across from the entrance to the famous Otesaga Hotel, and was sculpted and designed by Bostonian artist John Horrigan Sr. Dedicated on Armistice Day, 1931, and costing $4,000, the life-size soldier figure is incredibly detailed and has been hailed as one of the finest of its kind in the state. The statue stands atop a forty-ton pink granite boulder. A plaque affixed to it honors the memories of the natives of Cooperstown who fought and died in the First World War. It is poignant to see a familiar name among the list of fallen heroes: James Fenimore Cooper Jr.

It is amazing that two of America's great public sculptors, Victor Salvatore and Stanley Bleifeld, are responsible for five of Cooperstown's most alluring landmarks.

WHILE HERE

The National Baseball Hall of Fame is open year round (http://www.baseball halloffame.org) and has a fully active, revolving series of exhibits. (A word to the wise . . . summers are *extremely crowded* in tiny Cooperstown. It might be smart to plan your trip to the baseball shrine in the late spring or the autumn.) The Fenimore Art Museum, one mile up the west side of the lake on NYS Route 80, features paintings from the Hudson River School, an entire wing of rare Native American artifacts, plus ever-changing exhibits of early American masters (Frederic Church, Grandma Moses, Ansel Adams, and more). It is located at the site

of a Cooper family ancestral home on the shores of Lake Otsego (http://www
.fenimoreartmuseum.org). The Farmers' Museum (home of the Cardiff Giant and
the newly installed Empire Carousel) is located across the street from the art
museum. You can park at one place and walk to both (http://www.farmersmuseum
.org). Glimmerglass Opera is eight miles up NYS Route 80 from Cooperstown on
the lakefront. With some exceptions, their season runs July and August (http://
www.glimmerglass.org).

For a delightful surprise, a trip to the Fly Creek Cider Mill in nearby Fly
Creek is a wonderful and delicious experience of tastes and smells. This is one
of Upstate New York's most popular working cider mills, and taking home a jug
o' cider from Fly Creek is a longstanding tourist tradition in this area (five miles
west of Cooperstown; to view their facility or order products, visit http://www
.flycreekcidermill.com).

A trip down Main Street Cooperstown will expose you to everything
baseball, with no fewer than three dozen baseball memorabilia stores selling
everything from bobble-heads to team jerseys to priceless autographs. In the sum-
mertime, it is not unusual to find ballplayers from "the good old days" seated
behind a card table along the sidewalks signing autographs and dusting off old
baseball memories for curious bystanders. Walking tours are a popular way to
see Cooperstown, and most of them end up at writer Cooper's grave (http://www
.CooperstownWalks.com).

For lodging, dining, events, and more information contact the Cooperstown
Chamber of Commerce online at http://www.CooperstownChamber.org.

REFERENCE FILE

Dr. Louis C. Jones (1908–1990) was a renowned author, lecturer, professor, and
historian who served for many years as director of the New York State Historical
Association. His book *Cooperstown* (originally published by NYSHA in 1949; the
most recent edition was published by Farmers' Museum in 2006) is considered to
be a definitive work on the history of this famous village.

Although there is little to be found about sculpture Victor Salvatore online
(even though his obituary in the New York Times is fairly comprehensive), the
Web site http://www.AskArt.com features a short biography of him as well as
some photographs of his work.

7

"WE'LL NEVER FORGET THEM"

The Glass Workers' Tragedy Memorial, Corning

Corning, New York, is a bustling community of around 11,000 residents that appears to be a city much larger than it really is. It embraces small town values and lifestyles and yet is the home of several world-class venues that attract hundreds of thousands of visitors each year. The Village of Corning was established in 1848 and began pretty much as a speculative opportunity by (and for) Erastus Corning. Mr. Corning was a whirlwind of a man who was never content to confine himself to one avocation or hobby. He was a businessman (hardware, iron works), a land investor (personally owning more than 250,000 acres of land throughout several states), a magnate (he built the New York Central Railroad, at the time the largest corporation in America), and a politician (he was elected to the New York State Senate and the US Congress and also served as mayor of the city of Albany). His namesake city was one of his pride and joys.

Corning is known by all as the Glass Capital of the World and to some as the Crystal City. The glassworks was founded by the Houghton family of Massachusetts in 1851 and moved to its central New York locale a few years later (legendary actress Katherine Hepburn was a direct Houghton descendant). Clearly, the company is by and large the main employer of the region, and the area's economic health is inextricably tied to this Fortune 500 firm. More than 25,000 people work for the glassworks, not all of them here in Upstate New York.

Corning is a four-season paradise boasting beautiful, fragrant springs, warm lakeside summers, blazing autumnal bliss in the fall, and a multitude of snow-fun activities in winter. Sports are taken seriously in this rugged area of weather extremes, whether skiing, boating, or world-class golf. The Corning Classic, a

pivotal stop on the Ladies' Professional Golf Association Tour, has been held at the Corning Country Club ever since 1979. The winner of the 2007 tournament, Young Kim, took home $195,000 in first place prize money!

THE MEMORIAL

Glassworking has always been an accident-prone occupation, with fire, steel, and molten glass combining to make a combustible work environment, especially in the early days of the industry.

In 1891, a labor dispute at the Corning Glass Works sent seventy-five workers to a subsidiary plant in Findlay, Ohio, where there was a glassworker shortage. This group of Corning natives boarded an eastbound train in Findlay on July 3, 1891, for an excursion back home to be with their families for the July 4 celebration in the city of Corning. These employees were not just ordinary factory workers, but many of them were master craftsman in the delicate art of bulb-blowing. Shortly after the train pulled out of Findlay, while going through the community of Ravenna, Ohio, it was hit head-on by a speeding freight train with horrific results. The crash sent both trains telescoping into each other and the mayhem was extensive. The coach, which housed all of the glass workers, was in the rear of the train and was completely smashed and set ablaze. Nineteen of the Corning workers were pronounced dead at the scene. All of the others received varying degrees of injuries. It was the single worst accident in the history of the glass industry.

Solon Richardson, the owner of the Findlay plant, was vacationing on Lake Erie at the time of the accident, and when told about the tragedy, he directed that his own money be immediately sent to cover the medical expenses of all of the injured workers and ordered that special train arrangements be made to send the deceased workers back home for burial. He was shocked and stunned at the tragedy and when asked for a comment he reportedly could only say, "We'll never forget them."

The city of Corning received the sad news and prepared for a citywide display of mourning and grief. The train carrying the dead workers was met by a large crowd and funerals were held in quick succession at St. Mary's Cemetery in South Corning.

A massive granite monument was erected over their graves by the American Flint Glass Workers Union, of which all nineteen were members. This monument is truly impressive. It consists of a huge archway straddling the graves, on which a life-size statue of a glass worker stands, some twenty-five feet in the air. The details of the worker are exact and quite amazing, right down to the long blowpipe in his hands. All of the dead workers are identified on this memorial, giving both name and age at death (ages sixteen to twenty-six). It was designed and erected in 1892 by Riley Brothers Foundry of Brooklyn.

St. Mary's is a splendidly cared-for cemetery, and the Glass Workers' Tragedy Memorial is hard to miss, towering as it does over the landscape. The cemetery is located near the intersection of Park Avenue and Cemetery Road in South Corning. Make the second left inside the cemetery and you will see the memorial.

WHILE HERE

Clearly, the number one tourist attraction within miles of here is the Corning Museum of Glass (http://www.cmog.org). The museum (decidedly *not* a product placement ad for the Corning Glass Company, but more determinedly a museum of the history of *all* glass and glass making) holds invaluable, rare pieces of historic glass art and sculptures and welcomes nearly a third of a million visitors through its doors annually (and all of this in a city of only about 11,000!). The museum is a precious asset in this sometimes-struggling region of New York.

In June 1972, disaster struck the glass museum when Hurricane Agnes coaxed the roily waters of the nearby Chemung River out of its banks. Nearly five feet of putrid river water dumped into the museum, soaking the volumes in the library, smashing through priceless display cases, and ruining the infrastructure of the building. Experts called the flood "the greatest single catastrophe ever borne by an American museum." Through the Herculean efforts of the management, paid staff, and an army of volunteers, the museum reopened its doors to guests within an astonishing two months.

Another top-class attention-getter in Corning is the Rockwell Museum of Western Art (http://www.rockwellmuseum.org) at 111 Cedar Street (the old city hall). This beautiful facility holds a wondrous collection of masterpieces of the Old West by some of America's favorite artists. Donated to the city by Robert and Hertha Rockwell in 1976, the stars of this multimillion dollar collection are the many original works of Frederic Remington, Charles M. Russell, and Albert

Bierstadt. This popular tourist destination also features a well-stocked gift shop and a unique Southwestern-flavored eatery called the Cantina.

Around town, people watching and bargain shopping are the order of the day around the Gaffer District of the historic center city area. You will have plenty of dining choices there as well. But for a real adventure, utilize "the southern gateway to the Finger Lakes" as a wonderful jumping-off point to many of New York's best wineries, a large number of which are located within an hour of Corning. The region is stunning in all seasons with its gently rolling hills and pristine lakes, and the wineries, both big and small, offer much to see, taste, and learn during your visit here. A perfect place to begin your Corning-based wine region visit would be pretty little Hammondsport. An easy thirty-mile drive from Corning, the Hammondsport area is arguably the very heart of wine country, with nearly a dozen wineries of varying sizes to choose from nearby. "Wine-ing" is a natural pastime in this area, and to plot your daytrips out of Corning, visit the Web site http://www .newyorkwines.org and its very helpful Uncork New York! sites.

New York ranks third in wine and grape production in the United States (behind California and Washington), and the winery industry is a billion-dollar engine that drives the economy of the Finger Lakes Region. Following New York City and Niagara Falls, the wine country is the states third most sought after tourist destination.

REFERENCE FILE

A good starting point for those interested in the history of the Corning glass empire, *The Corning Museum of Glass: A Guide to the Collections* by Richard W. Price (Corning Museum of Glass, 2001) contains 192 pages of vivid, colorful photos and interesting text about the history of the Corning museum. It can be ordered online from the museum gift shop at http://www.cmog.org.

8

HELLMIRA

The Elmira Confederate Prison Monument, Elmira

Elmira, New York, straddles the Chemung River just north of the Pennsylvania state line, fifty miles west of Binghamton. The city lies entirely in the river's flood plain and has been devastated several times by the Chemung's torrents (the last, and worst, in 1972 following Hurricane Agnes). From the riverfront to the towering hills behind it, Elmira offers a curiously beautiful landscape for the visitor and musters up a quaint charm in an "olde tyme" way. Mark Twain lived here (and wrote here) for years and is the unofficial mascot of the city, but he is not the only esteemed American to call Elmira home. In fact, a sign at the entrance to the city, bannered "Honoring the Past; Building the Future," features the visages of several famous Elmirans: Brian Williams, NBC newsman; Hal Roach, movie legend and creator of *The Little Rascals*; Ernie Davis, the first African American Heisman Trophy winner; Samuel Clemens, who wrote as Mark Twain; Eileen Collins, an astronaut and the first female space shuttle commander; Sexton John W. Jones, a legendary conductor of the Underground Railroad; and Tommy Hilfiger, fashion designer. How's that for an A-list of former residents!

Elmira's downtown area offers several interesting eateries, pubs, and cafés, and in the summer the sidewalks are busy and animated. The Wisner Market, a longtime tradition, brings an abundant farmer's market to the business district on Thursdays in the summer months, and the riverfront is being developed for extended family use, such as concerts, fireworks, and boating events.

One of the major employers in the Queen City is the Elmira Correctional Facility. This maximum-security prison, known by locals as the Hill, houses around 350 criminals. Today it is a model prison in the New York State prison system.

THE MONUMENT

Because Elmira was located near the junction of major railroads and an early New York State canal (the Chemung Canal), it was a natural setting for the US Army to gather troops before sending them south to fight in the Civil War. Thousands of Union soldiers came through Western New York, and Elmira, during the early 1860s. But as the war ground on, the need for a training and mustering point lessened while the need for a prison camp grew. With the numbers of Confederate soldiers being captured increasing dramatically, the run-down thirty-acre facility at the army camp, then called Camp Rathbun, was pressed into service as a new, and one of the largest, Confederate soldier prisoner-of-war camps in the North. Officially known as Camp Elmira, it was known by those unlucky enough to serve time there as Hellmira. Many called it the worst prison camp ever constructed on American soil, even worse than the infamous Andersonville prison camp (Camp Sumter).

One in four southern prisoners imprisoned here breathed their last at Camp Elmira, an astounding statistic. Of the more than twelve thousand prisoners kept there, more than half suffered from disease and starvation. Open sewers, rotting food, a shortage of doctors, sweltering heat, raging floods (the prison camp was built alongside the cantankerous Chemung River), indifferent camp supervisors, and a lack of funds made life at Camp Elmira a nightmare.

In its first year of operation, due to severe overcrowding, nine hundred pris-oners were housed *out in the open* from the heat of July through the freezing cold of January. And this was at a time when Elmira was experiencing one of its worst winters on record. The messengers of death at Camp Elmira were typhoid, pneu-monia, and chronic diarrhea. The latter is listed as the cause of death on nearly one thousand death certificates alone. A sad subtext to the deaths of the nearly three thousand prisoners in the year the camp was operated is that malnutrition was a contributing factor in nearly all them. The irony is that Elmira is located in the heart of New York State's agricultural region, a place that has never seen a shortfall of meat or produce. Obviously, and records support the notion, this leads to the conclusion that the men were starved on purpose.

Each day, a hundred dead soldiers were loaded onto the oxcarts that carried them the mile and a half to Woodlawn Cemetery where they were buried. Sexton John W. Jones, an ex-slave and, one would think, no friend to the Confederate soldiers, dutifully recorded each man's name and rank and date of death before burial, an astonishing act of respect and humility that is still considered to be one of the most important burial recordings in America's history. Later, all military burials and reburials here, both North and South, were placed in the Woodlawn National Military Cemetery, adjacent to the public cemetery (and bordering the new Elmira State Penitentiary). With its designation as an official military burial ground, Woodlawn joins Albany, Bath, Calverton, Cypress Hills, Long Island, and Saratoga as the official resting place for New York's military personnel.

On July 15, 1864, a prison train bearing 833 Confederate prisoners-of-war (and 128 Union guards) was transferring the prisoners from a camp in Point Lookout, Maryland, to Camp Elmira. At 2:50 in the afternoon, the train, steam-ing through Shohola, Pennsylvania, slammed head on into a fifty-car coal train heading the opposite direction. The crash was horrific, destroying both trains and sending bodies flying through the air. By the time the toll was taken, 51 Confed-erate soldiers were dead, along with 17 Union guards. At the time it was the worst US train accident ever.

The Elmira Confederate Prison Monument is a solitary yet moving tribute to those who served and those who suffered at Hellmira. Situated within the boundaries of where the camp once was (no original structures exist), a panel tells the story of this awful moment in the city's history in words and photos. The multipaneled presentation sits amid a well-landscaped alcove in front of the Elmira wastewater treatment plant on the banks of the Chemung River. Enter Elmira on Route 352 (Church Street) and turn south on Foster Avenue just two blocks from the Walnut Street Bridge. Turn onto Winsor Street and you will see the memorial. One of the most poignant features of the memorial is that the Confederate Flag flies over the top of it, in solemn reverence to more than three thousand "sons of the South" who repose eternally in the Upstate New York city of Elmira.

WHILE HERE

Elmira is a city of wide boulevards, grand Victorian homes with large, well-manicured lawns, and a busy and interesting business district. History has been a frequent visitor to this city on the Chemung River, and the community embraces whole-heartedly the legend and mystique of its most famous resident, Mark Twain (Samuel Clemens). He first visited Elmira in the 1860s, and it was here that he married Olivia Langdon on February 2, 1870.

The author wrote at his sister-in-law's farm, Quarry Farm, on a hill just outside of Elmira for more than twenty years. In his unique, octagonal writing study there, Twain wrote *The Prince and the Pauper, The Adventures of Tom Sawyer, A Connecticut Yankee in King Arthur's Court, The Adventures of Huckleberry Finn,* and much more. Today, Twain's writing gazebo is permanently on display at Elmira College, which also holds many of Twain's personal artifacts. A vivid, life-sized statue of the writer is placed prominently on the campus.

The Clemens Center is the region's premiere entertainment venue, and one of the main roads in the city is named Clemens Center Parkway. Within the city limits is Woodlawn Cemetery. This cemetery, one of the most beautiful cemeteries in the Upstate New York region, holds the remains of many famous Americans, including Hal Roach, Ernie Davis, Sexton John W. Jones, and, of course, Mark Twain. (The cemetery has well-placed directional signs to all of the above graves.)

Adjoining the cemetery to the north is the National Military Cemetery (it has a separate entrance). Here are the graves of thousands of military dead. The Confederate dead from the Civil War–era Elmira prison are all in the same marked area. The Confederate dead from the Shohola train accident are noted with the addition of an "S" to their gravestone. A large bronze monument lists all of their names and mentions the details of the accident. Fittingly, all of the Union dead buried here are facing the north. The thousands of Confederate dead were buried facing the south.

Adjoining the national cemetery is the present-day Elmira Prison, an imposing facade of brick and barbed wire.

REFERENCE FILE

Elmira: Death Camp of the North by Michael Horigan (Stackpole Books, 2006) is an important work on this subject. The Internet has many sites regarding the Elmira camp, but none is as comprehensive as http://www.angelfire.com/ny5/ elmiraprison. Here you will find stories, maps, biographies, and archival photos of one of the deadliest prisoner-of-war camps in American history.

9

MIRACLE IN THE ADIRONDACKS

The Dr. Trudeau Memorial, Saranac Lake

The majestic Adirondack Mountains of Upstate New York are truly one of America's great treasures. It was the first publicly designated wilderness area in America (1892) and is the largest National Historic Landmark in the country.

With a size of 6.1 million square acres, the Adirondack State Park is larger than Yellowstone, Everglades, Grand Canyon, and Glacier National Parks combined! And remember, we are talking about a state park here. More than half of the park area is in private hands. Within the park's boundaries, the visitor will find hundreds of miles of paved and dirt roads, more than three thousand lakes, dozens of rivers plentiful with fish, and much more. This is Vacationland (as the ubiquitous 1950s-era bumper sticker used to say) after all, and in the heat of the summer—as well as in the blaze of autumn—the park area doubles in population as urban residents (mostly from Downstate) flee to the inland comforts of the Adirondacks for fun, recreation, and relaxation.

Many of the state's most charming and nostalgic little communities are found in the park. Dannemora, Long Lake, Tupper Lake, Old Forge, Corinth, Ticonderoga, Inlet, Lake Placid, Speculator, and others welcome visitors with (mostly) pristine lakes, quaint main streets, and a wistful sense of a vanishing Americana. Blue Mountain Lake is a must-stop destination for the first-time visitor. It is home to the wonderful Adirondack Museum and is the perfect introduction to this vast and historic region of New York State.

One of the prettiest communities in the entire region is Saranac Lake. This lake village (population around 5,000) has a long and rich history; many old, architecturally stunning buildings; and an active and vibrant community

organization. In the summer the sidewalks are buzzing with vacationing families, in the autumn the "leaf peepers" are dazzled by a crazy quilt of colors tinting the hills and mountains surrounding the village, and in the winter outdoor enthusiasts head here for skiing, snowshoeing, snowmobiling, ice skating, and more. Saranac Lake's Winter Carnival is one of the ten longest continuously running winter festivals in the United States—more than a century old.

At one time, the Queen of the Adirondacks was serviced by several railroads, boasted the largest and finest hotels in the region, rolled out the red carpet for the likes of President Calvin Coolidge and entertainer Al Jolson, was the hideaway of choice for scientist Albert Einstein, and was the place where a sickly writer named Robert Louis Stevenson penned his classic *The Master of Ballantrae* in 1889.

Although the many towns and villages of the Adirondack Mountain area may seem forgotten and well off the beaten path, some of them have been the sites of historic and important events throughout the years. Lake Placid, for example, with a population of only 2,700, hosted the Winter Olympics twice, in 1932 and 1980, and put this region on the map. Wilton, New York (population 12,000), is home of Mount McGregor, where President Ulysses S. Grant died while writing his memoirs in 1885. Eagle Bay is located at Big Moose Lake in the remote heart of lake country. Even though the population of the hamlet is less than 500 residents, it was the site of the murder of Grace Brown in 1906. This lurid tale of love and murder was turned into the classic 1925 novel by Theodore Dreiser, *An American Tragedy*. The murder (and the electrifying trial of her killer Chester Gillette) is still considered by many to be New York's crime of the century.

Blue Mountain Lake welcomes thousands of tourists and researchers each year to the Adirondack Mountain Museum, despite the fact that the population of Blue Mountain Lake is just 146 residents. The small village of Saranac Lake was the location of what many called the Miracle of the Adirondacks years ago (and I don't mean the USA ice hockey victory over the Russians at Lake Placid's Olympics in 1980, still known as the Miracle on Ice).

This "miracle" involved a lonely outsider, an insidious disease, the clean air of the mountains, and a small "cure cottage" called Little Red.

Edward Livingston Trudeau was born in New York City in 1848. Both of his parents were physicians, but that did not keep his family from being visited by sickness and disease over the years. His elder brother James contracted tuberculosis, which would kill him within three months of his diagnosis. Determined to follow in the footsteps of his parents, Edward enrolled in Columbia Medical College in 1868. Two years after his graduation in 1871, he also contracted tuberculosis and was pronounced gravely ill. With the TB vaccine still decades away, patients faced a difficult and ultimately grim path of treatment. The disease, which attacks the lungs and the nervous system, almost always resulted in death. But a new wave of natural treatment therapy, originating in Europe, was sweeping the crowded TB wards around the world, and more and more patients began to experiment with this basic, simple, and commonsense approach to curing the disease: fresh air!

As championed by Prussian doctor Hermann Brehmer, this holistic, simple approach to a previously untreatable disease called for large doses of rest, relaxation, and plenty of clean, cold mountain air. Dr. Robert Koch, a German bacteriologist, confirmed Brehmer's findings. Several physicians in the United States noted results of this "cure therapy," but test cases were few and far between. Dr. Trudeau decided that with his future bleak and uncertain, he would travel from the stifling surroundings of New York City to the high peaks region of New York's Adirondack Mountains, to spend what he thought were his final days on earth. He disembarked from the train at the Saranac Lake depot borne on a stretcher.

He checked into one of the grandest hotels in the region (Paul Smith's Hotel) and began practicing the ritual of cold mountain air, walks, and breathing therapy.

Amazingly, his tuberculosis went into remission.

Following his "cure," Dr. Trudeau moved into Saranac Lake and set up a practice for the treatment of tuberculosis. His first cure cottage, Little Red, was a tiny, two-room, bright red miniature Victorian house set on the grounds of his fledgling TB sanatorium. It cost $350 to build this first cottage. In May 1885, he welcomed his first visitors, Alice and Mary Hunt, two TB patients described as "poorly fed, frail and ill-clad factory girls" (the quoted material here was gathered from signs and plaques on the institute's grounds). They were soon cured, at no expense to themselves. Trudeau had decided early on that he would make his remedy available to all, including those "short on purse."

Word quickly spread throughout New England about the revolutionary new fight against the scourge of tuberculosis, and soon people from far and wide were making the trek to remote Saranac Lake for Dr. Trudeau's treatment. Cure cottages sprang up all over the grounds of his sanatorium and onto the hills around the town. Long wide porches dotted with special cure chairs, created especially for Dr. Trudeau's patients to relax in while in an upright position, became a familiar sight throughout the growing community. Millionaires and celebrities flocked to the Adirondacks, pinning their hopes on the Trudeau cure for rescuing them from tuberculosis.

Writer Robert Louis Stevenson, plagued with the disease since childhood, came for the cures and fell in love with the town. His Robert Louis Stevenson Cottage (44 Stevenson Lane, Saranac Lake) is preserved as a museum to his life and career. Christy Mathewson, known as the Big Six, a legendary baseball star who was a member of the initial induction class at the National Baseball Hall of Fame in Cooperstown, fought his valiant fight against tuberculosis here in the 1920s. He had been gassed during military training exercises in 1918 and contracted the disease from this accident. The New York Giants baseball legend died at a cure cottage in Saranac Lake, New York, on October 7, 1925.

By the early 1900s, Saranac Lake was the center for TB rehabilitation in the United States and acted as a model for cure communities all over the country. Villagers took in the overflow of Trudeau's sanatorium and added extra floors to their homes to house TB patients for profit. Many of these oddly proportioned homes, with the distinctive "cure porches" coming most often off the breeze-catching upper levels of their homes, are still recognizable in the village (52 and 135 Bloomingdale Avenue; and 134, 192, 211, and 247 Park Avenue, for example). Dr. Trudeau was hailed as a hero and a true medical pioneer.

He established the Adirondack Cottage Sanitorium [sic] and the Saranac Laboratory for the Study of Tuberculosis here in 1894, and ten years later he became the first president of the American Lung Association.

THE MEMORIAL

The impressive monument to Dr. Trudeau sits on the grounds of the Trudeau Institute at 154 Algonquin Avenue in Saranac Lake. The famous sculptor Gutzon Borglum (who also chiseled the iconic presidential visages on Mount Rushmore) portrayed in bronze an image of an ill Dr. Trudeau, well within the clutches of tuberculosis, huddled under a heavy blanket, languishing in his cure chair. Borglum positioned his subject facing out over the shimmering waters of a pristine lake. The sight is both majestic and poignant. The monument was dedicated on August 19, 1918, with a crowd of 1,500 former patients and family members in attendance. These former patients had all contributed to the cost of the memorial to the good doctor. Borglum, who admired Trudeau although he had met him just once, charged them only the cost of materials for the monument.

To get to the tribute to Dr. Trudeau, enter Saranac Lake on Route 3N (from the west). Just inside the village limits, you will see a small sign (*very* small) indicating the turn for the Trudeau Biomedical Research Institute. Turn left here, on Algonquin Avenue (it is a dead-end road, but pay no mind and go all the way to the end). At the end is the modern, impressive Trudeau Institute. A sign will direct you to the Dr. Trudeau Memorial out back. (A traveler's tip: If you have reached Saranac Lake High School on Route 3N while looking for the turn to the institute, you have gone too far.)

The institute is a secure workplace, so there is no public reception area to enter unaccompanied. However, you can peer inside through the giant windows and see the large lobby, with flags of the countries of the world ringing the atrium as well as the many awards and tributes to Dr. Trudeau and his descendants. The board of directors of the Trudeau Institute currently contains another in a long line of Dr. Trudeau's family members—great-grandson Gary Trudeau, the award-winning cartoonist of *Doonesbury* and a Saranac Lake native.

WHILE HERE

Before leaving the Trudeau Institute to explore the fun and activities of this Adirondack community, notice the little red house on the grounds of the institute, directly across the parking lot from the entrance. This is Little Red, the first cure cottage from 1885. You can go up on the porch and look in at the period furnishings, including the iron frame beds the two young women first rested on while recovering from tuberculosis. This is a fascinating glimpse at what was once Saranac Lake's biggest booming business, the cure cottages.

Notice the bronze plaque on the outside of the building, a historical marker telling of the preservation efforts to restore Little Red. The logo of the preservation group is the customized cure chair made for Dr. Trudeau and his patients.

A mile away, downtown Saranac Lake offers shopping, dining, and a whiff of 1950s nostalgia. The Hotel Saranac, which opened in 1927 as Upstate New York's first fireproof hotel, lords over the business district at six stories tall. Its second floor outside balcony allows a unique view of the town and its goings-on. Over the years, Saranac Lake has been voted by travel magazines as the number one small town in New York State and the number eleven small town in the United States. Mount Pisgah (elevation 2,080 feet) is Saranac Lake's popular ski resort. In the summer and fall, it offers the most sweeping view of Saranac Lake and the surrounding peaks and is a frequented area for picnics and gatherings.

REFERENCE FILE

An interesting book regarding Trudeau and his Miracle in the Adirondacks is *Cure Cottages of Saranac Lake: Architecture and History of a Pioneer Health Resort* by Philip L. Gallos (Historic Saranac Lake Association, 1985). There is much to be found on the Internet regarding Dr. Trudeau and the village of Saranac Lake. A helpful first stop is http://www.historicsaranaclake.org.

Clearly, Gutzon Borglum's magnum opus is his Mount Rushmore presidential tribute carved into the Black Hills of South Dakota. For the history of this national treasure (including images) visit http://www.nps.gov/moru/index.htm.

SAINT OR SINNER?

The John Brown Statue, Lake Placid

THE PLACE

Located in the town of North Elba, fifty miles south of the Canadian border, Lake Placid, New York, with a population of just 2,000 residents, may be the smallest (or certainly one of the smallest) communities ever to host an event of the magnitude of an international Winter Olympics. And it did it twice! Only the European villages of Innsbruck and St. Moritz have also hosted the Winter Olympics more than once. Both the 1932 and the 1980 Winter Olympiads were held here in the Adirondacks, bringing tens of thousands of visitors to the small winding roads and small, rural communities of the region (Lake Placid is not accessible by a major highway thoroughfare). Many of the original Olympic structures remain in use today, giving this northern village a decidedly alpine feel.

The main street is lined with stylish stores and restaurants, more on the high end than not. Ski supply stores, outerwear outlets, and shoe and boot stores number more than a dozen in the three-block downtown business district. Tony restaurants and comfortable inns make this locale one of the most visited spots in the Upstate New York area.

The views of the High Peaks, known as the Rockies of the East, from virtually every street corner are breathless, especially the glimpse of New York's own Mount Fuji, Whiteface Mountain, with its continuously snowcapped peak. Lake Placid is a stunning four-season resort community, with the fall color season especially becoming a competitor to the winter season for tourist dollars. The lake itself, which the village surrounds, is deep, cold, and clear and filled with dozens of islands. These islands are home to many lovely (and expensive) lake cottages

with lawns rolling down to the water, wide sweeping sitting porches, and distinctive Adirondack-style boathouses.

Gerrit Smith (of Peterboro, near Syracuse) was a social reformer, a wealthy businessman, and one of the leading voices (and monetary supporters) of abolition. He was a landowner with many thousands of acres to his name, and he came to the town of North Elba in 1845 to buy up more land. Ultimately, Smith gave away large portions of his land to three thousand African Americans for a community named Timbuctoo, just outside present-day Lake Placid. John Brown, a dynamic personality with like-minded antislavery sentiments, arrived here (with his wife and seven of their children) in May 1849 to join Smith in hopes of beginning a "Freed Slave Utopian Experiment" of black and white people living together in harmony. Brown hoped this self-sufficient, free (and voting) community would spark a wave of similar communities across the liberal north. Although the land was notoriously inhospitable to farming, Timbuctoo was a measured success for a brief period, and many African American residents of present-day Essex and

Franklin counties can directly trace their heritage back to this black enclave just outside Lake Placid.

John Brown began his noble quest for the end of slavery as a speaker and rabble-rouser and eventually spiraled into a quixotic mission that included violent ends to accompany his violent means. Even President Lincoln, once a supporter, ended up referring to Brown as a "lunatic." A leader of the Bleeding Kansas Raids in the mid-1850s, Brown's reign of violence ended with his ill-conceived attack on the federal armory in Harper's Ferry, West Virginia, to gain arms for his insurrections. Brown and his raiders, including some family members, were caught, arrested, convicted, and hanged for their crimes. They are buried in a small grave on his property. John Brown's grave is encased in glass, as years of Adirondack winters have taken a toll on the carvings and epitaph inscribed on it.

THE STATUE

After John Brown's death, his family and a few black supporters carried on at the North Elba farm, but eventually, their numbers dwindled and they moved to California. The property was transferred to New York State in 1896 and ultimately purchased by the John Brown Association. The home and grave are New York State and National Historic Landmarks. On May 9, 1935, a heroic statue of John Brown, his arm draped around a young African American boy, was unveiled with much ceremony. The boy looks up at Brown with admiration and love, as the old man strides forcefully along, gesturing and orating. It is a large, strong statue and really captures the messianic personality of Brown as well as the subtle tenderness he felt toward the black people whom he lived with and aided over the years.

Sculptor Joseph Pollia (1893–1954) created a brash fifteen-foot memorial to Brown, and the setting of the statue is unique. Brown's original house and farm as well as his grave can be seen behind it. In front of the grave, however, is a barren field, perhaps indicative of the harsh farming conditions met by Brown and his followers. Just north of the statue, but in plain view, is the modern, jarring, and quite out of place Olympic ski jump, used in the 1980 Winter Olympics. The towering ski jump, seen in the same visual frame as the statue, makes for one of the most disconcerting contrasts encountered in researching this book.

Pollia's other famous sculpture is My Buddy, a famous World War I bronze Doughboy erected in Forest Park, Queens.

WHILE HERE

A walk along Main Street will take you past several plazas featuring Adirondack chairs on which you can sit and enjoy the view of the lake. You will stroll by a real nostalgic icon from America's past: a Howard Johnson's restaurant! The once ubiquitous orange-roofed eatery is no longer the staple of vacation-going families as it was in the past. In fact, with the complete dissolution of the company a few years ago, the number of restaurants went from more than six hundred to the present-day three, one in Bangor, Maine, one in Lake George, New York, and the last one, at 98 Saranac Avenue, here in Lake Placid!

The entire High Peaks region is a wondrous playground for outdoor activities, including fishing, hiking, skiing, snowmobiling, horseback riding, biking, and more. A hundred lakes are within an hour of Lake Placid, and the many tall mountains ringing the village are indeed as close as they look. For those more inclined to sitting rather than sweating, the picture-postcard village offers a leisurely experience in relaxed dining, window-shopping, and antiquing.

The Olympic Village still retains the glory of the 1932 and 1980 spotlights, and many of the original Olympic venues are intact, open to the public, and in daily use. The Olympic Arena, where the underdog American hockey team led by Herb Brooks crafted the 1980 Miracle on Ice defeat of the Soviets, is still open and now named after Brooks. For an older generation, this same ice-skating rink is where an unknown Sonja Henie won the second of her three consecutive gold medals at the 1932 Olympiad. The arena (located just off the downtown business district) also hosts the Lake Placid Winter Olympics Museum, with artifacts on display and revolving exhibits for adults and children of all ages. The skating rink is open to the public, and there is no greater thrill for young, aspiring skaters than to lace up and take a quick turn around the Herb Brooks Rink, under the big banner that reads "Home of the Miracle on Ice," all the while pumping their little arms in the air yelling "USA! USA! USA!" It happens there all the time!

Just outside of the village (at the John Brown Historic Site) are the Olympic Ski Jumps. These twin ninety- and one-hundred-twenty-meter towers are the tallest objects between Albany and Canada. Used constantly in the winter by practicing jumpers, the towers feature elevators and observation decks, which afford the absolute best mountain views in the entire Adirondack State Park.

For the ultimate in Olympic thrills, however, travel just a short distance (eight miles) from the village to Mount Van Hoevenberg, where bobsled experts from around the world practice. These flashy sleds scream down the ice troughs of the mountain at breakneck speed and offer some of the most thrilling moments in Winter Olympic history. A professional driver and a professional brakeman will sandwich you onto the sled and take you for the thrill of a lifetime down the mountain at blurring speeds. Though not for scaredy-cats, this experience has been called Lake Placid's greatest thrill ride!

For information on all of the original Olympic venues, visit the New York State Olympic Regional Developmental Authority online at http://www.orda.org/newsite.

Kate Smith, famous for singing "God Bless America," was one of America's greatest entertainers in the past century. A pioneer in both radio and television, Kate spent more than forty summers here in Lake Placid, and she is remembered by villagers with great fondness and nostalgia. Kate left her estate to her parish church, St. Agnes Catholic Church, just two blocks off Main Street at 169 Hillcrest Avenue. A plaque and large color portrait of the star adorns the entranceway to the church. A plaque to her memory is located on Main Street near the Olympic Center, and a street nearby is named after her. The Kate Smith Commemorative Society, the late singer's large fan club, holds a growing festive gathering here each year in her honor (http://www.KateSmith.org). Kate is buried at St. Agnes Cemetery (at the intersection of Olympic and Sentinel Avenues) in a giant, pink mausoleum. It is easily found, as it is the only mausoleum ever allowed in the cemetery. The gold inscription inside the glass doors of the tomb echoes the words of President Franklin D. Roosevelt: "This is Kate Smith. This is America." Her gravesite one of the most visited sites in Lake Placid.

REFERENCE FILE

To get a real perspective of the Lake Placid area, both now and in the past, a good source is the book *Lake Placid: Then and Now* by Laura Viscome (Arcadia Publishing, 2008). The book compares current scenes with past visages by creatively using current and old photographs and postcards. The text includes a wide sweep of Lake Placid's history.

An unusual look into the life of John Brown can be found at the Internet site http://www.JohnBrown.org. Here is the story of Brown and his family and followers and their arrival at the Kennedy Farmhouse in Maryland. Here they presented themselves as Mr. Isaac Smith and sons, New York cattle ranchers. The ruse was successful and the farm would ultimately become the launching place for their infamous raid on the Harper's Ferry arsenal. The Kennedy Farmhouse is today a National Historic Landmark.

near present-day Fort Ticonderoga, along the lake. Sensing he would
[bet]ter chance at victory if the Indians were without their leaders, he had a
[sho]t out the three Iroquois chiefs leading the war party. The legend is that
[he] killed two of the chiefs with a *single rifle shot* and sent the remaining
[fle]eing into the woods.

[Cham]plain roamed at free will the area known as New France (about a full
[third of] day's Canada) and was the first European to set foot in many of those
[area]s hailed today both in Canada and his native France as a rugged, heroic,
[my]thic figure of the New World, and statues, monuments, and memorials
[exist] in North America dedicated to his memory. The statue in Quebec is
[Can]ada's most treasured historic sites. Champlain died there on Christmas
[Day, and] the church where his body was interred burned to the ground in 1640,
[his re]mains were lost forever. Magnificent, impressive monuments to Cham-
[plain can] be found all around "his lake," including beautiful ones in Plattsburgh,
[Charlo]tte (Vermont), Champlain, and South Hero (Vermont).

[But her]e, the most beautiful and unforgettable monument to this statuesque
[man is at] Crown Point, New York.

THE MEMORIAL

[From 1]858, the Crown Point Lighthouse stood guard along the narrow slip of
[land bet]ween New York and Vermont for nearly seventy years. Originally just
[a run-of-th]e-mill lighthouse, with a tall, plain octagonal tower topped by a light
[at its eig]hty-three-foot-tall peak (a light that could be seen more than fifteen
[miles awa]y), the sturdy lighthouse performed perfectly throughout its career,
[keeping g]oods-laden ships away from the narrow rocky shores to safety. Ferries
[crossed b]etween the two states here, and the lighthouse and the little Cape
[Cod shac]k attached to it for the keeper became a popular and familiar sight for
[those p]assing through. When a new bridge spanning Lake Champlain was
[built in 1]929 (just feet from the Crown Point lighthouse), the keeper's house
[was torn] down and the light was decommissioned. This bridge was the first
[span cro]ssing between the two states and basically was the end to active Lake
[Champlai]n lighthouses. But something happened at Crown Point in 1919 that
[gave] the old lighthouse a new lease on life and let it shine well into the
[twenty-fir]st century.

11

VIVE LA FRANCE!
The Crown Point Lighthouse, Crown Point

THE PLACE

Crown Point is a small village in a very remote section of Upstate New York.
It has a population of fewer than 2,000, and even though it juts out into Lake
Champlain, the easternmost border to the town is the westernmost border of
Addison County, Vermont. Many residents of Crown Point commute to work in
Vermont, and until recently a bridge at Crown Point connected the two states.
However, the bridge was demolished in 2009 when it was found to be unsafe.
A new bridge is currently under construction. Both the French and the British
built large forts here in the late 1700s, as the region became a much fought-over
location because of the proximity of Crown Point to the narrow shipping lanes
of Lake Champlain. The views of Lake Champlain, particularly from the Crown
Point Memorial Lighthouse, are gorgeous.

New York State boasts some of the most beautiful and historic lakes in the
United States. They vary in size, are almost exclusively in Upstate New York, and
offer much history of New York and the nation itself. For example, Lake Otsego
in Cooperstown is the pristine nine-mile-long lake that is the backdrop for many
of James Fenimore Cooper's Leatherstocking Tales. Cooper referred to the lake
as "the Glimmerglass," a moniker still used by locals. The seven Finger Lakes
in Western New York offer a rich and important history encompassing everything from the founding of the women's rights movement to the operation of the
Underground Railroad to the birth of the now-burgeoning New York State wine
industry (with more than two hundred Finger Lakes wineries, the region is one
of the nation's leading wine producers). Canadarago Lake, just south of Richfield

Springs, has been called New York's cleanest lake. Onondaga Lake in Syracuse has been called its most polluted.

The Great Sacandaga Lake in Fulton County, a vacation destination so popular it was once called the Coney Island of the North, was created in the 1920s as a flood control project. Nearly three hundred million gallons of water flooded the river valley, creating a truly *great* Sacandaga Lake! High in the North Country, tiny Lake Tear in the Clouds is the starting point of the mighty Hudson River's 315-mile journey from the Adirondacks to the Statue of Liberty in New York harbor. Lake Ontario, one of the Great Lakes, forms the western shore of the state, and roughly two million New Yorkers live along this, Upstate's own "seashore."

Lake George, in Warren County, is one of New York's favorite vacation destinations, and Chautauqua Lake, in the county of the same name, is the site of the internationally famous writers' colony, the Chautauqua Institute. And Mud Lake? Well, take your pick: There are thirty-one different lakes officially named Mud Lake, scattered over sixteen different New York counties!

The lakes of New York, both big and small, h
and historical component of the state's heritage. A
role in this heritage than Lake Champlain.

Lake Champlain is a huge freshwater lake,
long and twelve miles wide. It forms the natural
Vermont. Burlington, Vermont (population 39,0
lake. The largest city on the New York side is P
The vistas (both east and west) are breathtaking
along the lake thrive in the summer season in a
just four lake crossings, and the ferry from Port K
one of the most pleasurable one-hour ferry trips
islands dot the lake, and far from being placid,
than not a body of water dancing with wind-whip

During the Revolutionary War, Lake Cha
several major battles. Fort Ticonderoga, sitting
Lake George, is one of the most imposing and s
War forts in the nation. The scene of several maj
known for what happened there on May 10, 177
patriots Ethan Allen, Benedict Arnold, and th
Vermont) strode through the unlocked, unguard
fort and captured the British garrison asleep in i
allowed for the transportation of Ticonderoga's
port the American siege of that British-controlle
told in chapter 17.) On October 11, 1776, the firs
on Lake Champlain. With the navy under the co
American victory over the British fleet on Lake
the ultimate defeat of the British later at Saratog
on Lake Champlain is considered to be the very
American navy.

Samuel de Champlain (1568–1635) was a F
dier, and mapmaker who discovered this lake in
of Quebec and Montreal, Canada. The explorer
between the fractious Indian tribes of the area
degree. When he did have to do battle, he was a
On July 29, 1608, Champlain and his small party

of Iroquo
have a be
scout poi
Champla
Indians fl

Char
third of t
areas. He
almost m
are prolif
one of Ca
Day, 1635
and his re
plain can
Isle de M

To n
man is at

Built in 1
water bet
a run-of-
at the ei
miles aw
steering
crossed
Cod shad
travelers
built in
was torn
bridge cr
Champla
would gi
twenty-f

On the three-hundredth anniversary of his birth, a committee was formed to look for suitable ways to honor Samuel Champlain. It was decided that a fitting memorial to the discoverer of the lake would be to turn the Crown Point Lighthouse into his memorial. With a gift of $50,000 from the Champlain Tercentenary Committee, eight stylish Doric columns were erected around the light tower, giving it a decidedly classical ambiance. The limestone base was removed and a solid granite foundation was put in its place. Many florid and impressive adornments add flavor to the structure, and depictions of the explorer and his adventures were carved around the tower's midsection. An elaborate "cage" for the beacon at the top was created. It became a beautiful (if unrecognizable) lighthouse doubling as a tribute to the great Frenchman.

Carl Heber, the American sculptor, created a brazen, forceful bronze image of Champlain studying "his lake," accompanied by a French soldier and an Indian guide. The statue seems to emerge from the side of the lighthouse. Champlain is in full armor, which is quite accurately detailed. The explorer's canoe juts out two feet from the exterior wall. Remarkably, an original Auguste Rodin sculpture is placed on the memorial just below Champlain's canoe. This was a gift of the master French artist and the nation of France. At the dedication of the Rodin bust on May 3, 1912, the French national representative said, "The United States is raising a monument to a Frenchman, and France sends you, through me, her special tribute of gratitude. Once more the two democracies are thinking and acting in unison." President William Howard Taft presided over the official dedication of the monument on July 5, 1912.

All in all, the majestic, towering lighthouse (still lit today for aesthetic reasons), situated along the shore of the beautiful blue waters of Lake Champlain with the Green Mountains of Vermont as a backdrop (and an original Rodin sculpture to boot!), add up to make this a sentimental and enduring place of history and beauty in Upstate New York.

WHILE HERE

This area is one of the most remote areas of any statue, monument, or memorial place in this book. The lighthouse is four miles north of the village of Crown Point in a sparsely populated area. A popular public campsite surrounds the Crown Point Lighthouse, and a covered viewing and fishing dock at the water's edge offers a stunning view at dusk of the twinkling lights of Vermont across the water. The lighthouse's circular stairway allows the visitor to go to the top for a spectacular view. Warning: Do not go into the lighthouse at night unless you want to be in the company of several dozen bats. I learned the hard way!

Directly across the entrance road to the lighthouse is the main gate for the Crown Point Historic Site. Here are the ruins of the British-held Fort St. Frederic, which in 1742 was the largest British fort of its kind anywhere in North America. When the French pushed the British out during the French and Indian War, the French torched the fort, but the British built a new one, naming it Fort Crown Point. The huge cannons placed at these forts could reach Vermont, thereby controlling all comings and goings here at the narrowest point of the lake. Both forts remain in the shape of stone ruins and make for an interesting adventure while visiting the lighthouse. The ruins and the lighthouse are both operated by the Bureau of Historic Sites in the NYS Office of Parks, Recreation and Historic Preservation (http://nysparks.state.ny.us/historic-sites/34/details.aspx).

REFERENCE FILE

New York has more lighthouses than any other state except Michigan. A fascinating look at all of them (with Crown Point being featured) is *New York State Lighthouses* by Robert G. Müller (Arcadia Publishing Co., 2006). The book has many archival photos of the lighthouses as well as facts about their construction, purpose, and locations.

Carl Heber (1875–1956) was a German American sculptor famous for his many war memorials. Crown Point was a distinct departure for him. Among his most famous works is the giant equestrian statue of Civil War General Philip Sheridan located in the soldier's hometown of Somerset, Ohio. Crown Point Lighthouse also features a bust by the legendary French artist Auguste Rodin. The most definitive Internet resource for everything Rodin is at http://www.rodin-web.org.

12

THE ULTIMATE SACRIFICE
The Gold Star Mother Memorial, Kent

THE PLACE

The southeastern corner of Upstate New York, the area just north of New York City and situated hard on the border of Connecticut, is a bucolic masterpiece of green rolling hills, small pre–Revolutionary War towns and villages, highlands offering stunning vistas of the nearby Hudson River, and history, history, history!

Putnam County is a jewel. It was named for Revolutionary War hero General Israel Putnam. The general, who was born just across the Connecticut border, not far from Kent, New York, was one of those classic, larger-than-life characters whose story is exciting, exaggerated, and unforgettable. A fierce patriot, the general, upon hearing of the start of the Battle of Lexington, left his plow in the field, suited up, and rode more than one hundred miles in eight hours to join the colonists. A natural and forceful leader, many think it was Putnam who gave the famous order, "Don't shoot until you see the whites of their eyes, boys!" at the Battle of Bunker Hill (although don't tell that to the descendants of Col. William Prescott, who believe that he gave us that immortal quote). He went on to be the full commander of the American troops throughout the state until the arrival of the new commander, General George Washington.

The colorful "Old Put" was a successful tavern keeper, which gave him a convivial arena to spin his tales of being the first person to bring tobacco seeds back from Cuba (his Connecticut shade leaf is still the premier cigar wrapper of choice by the top tobacco manufacturers) or of being captured by Indians and then being saved from being burned at the stake by them at the very moment the pyre was lit. Perhaps the most vivid larger-than-life tale told of and by Putnam was the fact that he was the man who used his bare hands to kill the last surviving wolf in the

state of Connecticut. A historical marker in Mashamoquet Brook State Park in Pomfret, Connecticut, tells this story and marks the cave where the last unfortunate she-wolf met extinction.

Quite a guy, huh?

Putnam County has many monuments honoring people and events of the Revolutionary War era and the typical town square memorials to the dead of all wars. But in the Putnam County Veterans Memorial Park in Kent there stands a slight memorial more eloquent (to me) than that of any braided general on a giant horse, more powerful than any Civil War cannon placed on a village green, more touching than any eternal flame, and more poignant than any other entry in this book.

It is a statue of a little lady, standing in her living room at the darkest moment of her life. It is, quite simply, unforgettable.

THE MEMORIAL

When we think of the Revolutionary War memorials we immediately think of the Minuteman on Lexington Green. When we think of the tributes to the Civil War we think of the hundreds of huge, blocky memorials dotting the landscape at Gettysburg. When we think of the tributes to World War II who cannot imagine the giant statue in Arlington, Virginia, of the US Marines struggling to raise the flag at Iwo Jima? Korea brings us to the chiseled, haunting images of the hollowed-eyed soldiers marching through a rice paddy as depicted in the Korean War Memorial in Washington, DC. Vietnam has its wall. When we think of tributes to the presidents, are we not impressed with the Lincoln Monument, Mount Rushmore, and Grant's Tomb? But this tiny little tribute, to a tiny little woman, located here in tiny little Kent, is the first of its kind in the United States to bestow honor upon a group of Americans who were also present (albeit from afar) at El Alamein and Bastogne and Hue and San Juan Hill and Inchon and Kirkuk and Midway Island and Normandy and Cantigny and Flanders Field. This touching tribute pays a long overdue respect and thanks to the mothers of the dead soldiers who gave their blood on unpronounceable battlefields around the globe in the name of their country.

They are the Gold Star Mothers.

On June 4, 1928, the first official meeting of the Gold Star Mothers organization took place in Washington, DC. Its founder, Grace Darling Seibold, had lost her son in 1918 in France, and his body was never recovered. With a sense of empty grief evolving into a sense of compassionate activism, Grace Seibold reached out to other mothers who had lost sons and organized them into comfort groups in support of each other. The group took its name from the gold star emblems hung in windows when a soldier son was killed. They commit themselves to work in veteran's hospitals, encourage the American spirit among the young of the nation, create a fellowship among all mothers who have children in the service, and act in any and all manner at the behest of veterans organizations. The organization grew to thousands of members after World War II. The last Sunday in September is Gold Star Mother's Day, designated by presidential proclamation. There are currently around 1,000 members of the group nationally. Membership is open to any mother or stepmother who has lost a child in the service of their nation.

The sculpture, by Andrew Chernak, a Vietnam veteran, is located in Putnam County Veterans Memorial Park in Kent. The Gold Star Mother stands on a massive pentagonal polished black granite pedestal with a large five-point gold star on the front. The image depicted is excruciating. A diminutive woman, clearly a World War II era mother, clutches a wrinkled piece of paper, obviously a Western Union telegram bringing bad news. The shocked mother turns away, her tear-streaked face lost and afraid. She braces herself against a small 1940s-era telephone table with spindly wooden legs. The table holds a photo of her soldier son, smiling out at her in his crisp uniform. The spilled and broken flowerpot lying on its side evidences the moment of shock. The tableau is frozen in time and is powerfully delivered in bronze.

Chernak's monument always brings a reverent silence from the onlooker. The model for this Gold Star Mother is the sculptor's wife, Terria. The statue is life-sized (5 feet 7 inches), and the World War II era dress on the model was sewn by Mrs. Chernak in two days. A Fountain of Tears will be installed in front of the monument in the near future. The three granite benches surrounding the statue offer a place for quiet reflection. The total cost of the statue and the surrounding setting was $50,000.

WHILE HERE

Two entries in *Monumental New York!* are within a ten-minute drive of each other, and I strongly advise that visitors see both. The Gold Star Mother Memorial is a mere eight miles away from the Sybil Ludington Statue in Carmel. Both offer wonderful characterizations of the effort made by women in our country's battles and sacrifices.

While visiting the Putnam County Veterans Memorial Park, there are a couple of other sights to see. On the upper level of the park (on the main road) you will pass a tribute to Daniel Nimham, one of the most famous area Indians. He was the most influential chief of his time and led his Wappinger tribe to a great role in the Hudson Valley. Nimham fought determinedly for the land of his people to be returned to them by the white man, but was unsuccessful. He was a courageous warrior who fought with Washington at Valley Forge and later died in battle (Kingsbridge, now Van Cortlandt Park in New York City). A monument in the park in the Bronx pays tribute to Nimham and his fifty warriors who died with him fighting the British for independence.

On the day I visited the Putnam County Veterans Memorial Park, its 225 acres were a beehive of summer activity. Families were enjoying summer picnics, volleyball games were being played, kids were flying kites, and dog walkers were pacing the woodland trails. In jarring juxtaposition to all of this, an M60A3 Army tank sat nearby, with a huge Cobra helicopter somehow suspended over it. Having never seen either of these pieces of weaponry, I was surprised at how large both were.

The park is located at 201 Gipsy Trail Road in Kent.

REFERENCE FILE

An interesting and little known story about the Gold Star Mothers concerns the time of their voyages following World War I. Thousands of women were escorted to Europe to visit the graves of their dead soldier sons and husbands. This fascinating tale is told in *The Gold Star Mother Pilgrimages of the 1930s: Overseas Grave Visitations by Mothers and Widows of Fallen U.S. World War I Soldiers* by John W. Graham (McFarland and Company, 2005).

To see examples of sculptor Andrew Chernak's work, visit http://www.old gloryprints.com.

THE FEMALE PAUL REVERE

The Sybil Ludington Statue, Carmel

Carmel, New York, is located in the verdant rolling hills of the lower Hudson Valley, where urban begins to give way to rural, where "city" transforms into "country," and where all roads east lead to Fairfield County, Connecticut (just one town away). New England begins to manifest itself here in the lower corner of Putnam County, where the gray of the urban macadam begins to surrender to the green of the suburban landscape and Revolutionary War history can be witnessed at every turn. Carmel itself is named after the biblical Mount Carmel, and the county is named in honor of Revolutionary War general Israel Putnam. Although Carmel is a bedroom suburb of New York City (an hour away), this community of 30,000 reaches back to its founding in 1740 to retain its small town ways, ideals, and values.

Its majestic, four-columned county courthouse, almost two hundred years old, is the second oldest operating courthouse in the state. Its lake, Lake Gleneida, is human-made and was created by a pair of brothers, the Smadbeck brothers, by damming up an old, fetid swamp and selling off the new "lakeside parcels." Rev. and Mrs. Norman Vincent Peale founded and headquartered their worldwide publication *Guideposts* here in 1945, and today the company has a stable of publications with a circulation of more than 4.5 million. Their first magazine was a four-page booklet with a story in it by World War I ace Eddie Rickenbacker. A fire devastated its circulation office, and famed newsman Lowell Thomas led a successful public drive to raise funds for the rebuilding of the publication's destroyed headquarters. (Thomas and the Peales were neighbors in the nearby hamlet of Quaker Hill.)

Carmel is a wealthy community where the median incomes are high. In fact, Putnam County is the tenth wealthiest county in America, with a median household income of $78,000 annually. The county has myriad high-ranked school districts and respected medical facilities, and it is home to many Fortune 500 CEOs and business leaders. But with this good life comes a weather oddity: Carmel (and all of Putnam County) lies within a dangerous tornado alley, something highly unusual in New York and New England. Situated between the rough-hewn valleys of the Hudson River to the west and the rising mountains of Connecticut to the east, Carmel has paid a dear price for its physical location.

Although the community has been plagued with rogue storms for decades (Carmel has a 25 percent higher tornado occurrence chance than the rest of the state), two in particular severely tested the mettle of longtime locals. On July 10, 1989, a devastating tornado visited Carmel. On July 29, 1997, a bigger Category 2 tornado (highest possible winds of 157 mph) tore through town. Damage totals for both of these recent storms went high into the millions of dollars. On August 22, 2000, a highly unusual 2.5 magnitude earthquake rumbled through Carmel, rattling windows and nerves throughout the city.

The area around Carmel and the entire county is rich with history, which leads us to "the little girl and her horse." In April 1777, the Revolutionary War was raging on various fronts throughout the Northeast. On the afternoon of April 26, British General William Tryon and his Redcoats came up from their ships on Long Island Sound and attacked, sacked, and burned Danbury, Connecticut. Clearly, the state line and the neighboring New York communities of eastern Putnam County were next in his sights. Word reached the Fredericksburg (now Ludingtonville) home of Henry Ludington, a colonel in the patriot militia, that the enemy was massing in Danbury, just twenty miles to the east. Sybil, the sixteen-year old eldest (of twelve) Ludington child, prevailed on her father to let her ride her horse, Star, through the countryside to alert her father's far-flung soldiers to gather and march on the British.

In the dark of the stormy night, on back roads that were no more than dirt paths (some of them uncharted), Sybil raced through the woods and valleys from farmhouse to town house, rallying her father's troops. She spurred Star on using a tree branch, rode sidesaddle since she was still too small to fit properly in a riding saddle, and covered more than forty miles in just a few hours (twice the distance covered by Paul Revere on his much more famous ride). Leaving behind a trail of flickering candles in windows and the echoing of the little towns' alarm bells, she rode on farther and faster down Horse Pond Road and on to Mahopac, Shaw's Pond, what is now the town of Kent, and Stormville. Along the way, she spotted rogue British patrols, at which point she would dismount and walk Star into the deep woods so as not be discovered.

At the beginning of her midnight ride, she went to each house and banged on the front door until someone answered her call. Realizing that most of the people were asleep and that this method was taking too much of her time, she finished her ride by just pulling up to the homes, rearing her horse, and yelling her warnings at the top of her lungs. The soldiers (more than four hundred) rallied with Col. Ludington near the state border at dawn and then marched on Danbury, where they successfully routed the British and sent them fleeing back to their ships.

The story of the young heroine raced up and down the Putnam/Dutchess County corridor, and soon people started to seek out the teenager to heap praise and honor on her. Even General Washington came to the Ludington home to pat the head of the "little girl on the horse." No dramatic essay can accurately capture the feelings little Sybil must have had as she and her trusty Star raced through the thunder and lightening of that evening more than 225 years ago, hiding in the dark from the enemy, and screaming at the top of her lungs for the soldiers to "come out and fight with her father." The word "heroic" doesn't seem adequate to describe what this "female Paul Revere" did that evening.

Perhaps the greatest tribute to this legendary figure is the electrifying statue of her and Star in mid-ride, created by Anna Hyatt Huntington.

THE STATUE

The tribute to this young heroine is dynamic. Sybil is seated on her steed side-saddle, her short legs barely reaching the horse's midsection. She is wielding a stick to prod her horse onward. Her face is full of expression and her eyes wide open; her hair flies in the wind and her mouth is agape, as if she were in mid-scream. Her horse is rearing under the strain of the tight-reined grip of its rider. The statue is three-dimensional and then some! You can feel the wind, hear the hoof beats, and sense the excitement of the moment.

The statue is situated on Route 52 at Lake Gleneida in Carmel (across the street from St. James Catholic Church). The beautiful lake makes a stunning, pastoral backdrop that contrasts mightily with the animated tones of the rider. Colorful plantings, a wall of spruce trees, and a New York State historical marker all highlight this incredible memorial. It is a tribute both to the high-flying spirit of the young girl as well as to the genius of the sculptor that this monument is considered to be one of the most popular public art pieces in America.

Anna Hyatt Huntington, the sculptor, was the most prolific female artist of her kind in America. Her huge, visceral pieces grace public venues from coast to coast. In 1923 Anna Hyatt married millionaire Archer Huntington, adopted son of the railroad magnate Collis P. Huntington. In 1931 Archer purchased thousands of acres of lush woodlands near Charleston, South Carolina, to erect a modern studio for his wife to work in and to build a private home and museum they could retreat to. Brookgreen Gardens welcomes thousands of visitors each year to view the mansion and stroll the remarkable sculpture garden featuring many of Anna's pieces. She was famous for creating bronze casts of muscle-taut horses straining at the reins and dramatic physical scenes taken from real life.

Among her most famous works of art (after the popular Sybil Ludington memorial) are her tributes to José Martí in New York's Central Park, her depiction of El Cid in San Diego, California, and her famous Holy Family Resting: Flight to Egypt at the National Cathedral in Washington, DC. One of her most interesting and intricate sculptures is the funereal tribute to her husband's stepmother, Arabella Huntington, at the extravagant Huntington mausoleum in Woodlawn Cemetery, Bronx. It features three mysterious life-sized figures: two of them are naked figures and the third a darkly shrouded "angel" guarding the crypt!

WHILE HERE

The attraction here *is* the area itself. In all four seasons, Putnam County sparkles. My best suggestion for a weekend visit is to simply take a drive. A leisurely spin through the little towns all around southern Putnam County makes for one of the most enjoyable "vacations" in the state. Traffic is not at the choking level yet, like it is in some of the small communities up and down the Hudson Valley. The towns here are just a couple of miles apart, unlike Western New York where you can go miles and miles in between towns. The roads are easy to drive, unlike some of the back roads in the Adirondacks where the journey is spoiled to a degree because you *have* to keep your eyes focused on the winding road ahead rather than on the majestic mountains and stunning beautiful lakes on either side of the road.

The communities are ancient and historic in their own right. Kent, for example, was founded in 1795, and Patterson, in 1798. Little Cold Spring is reported to have been named by George Washington himself, after he sipped from a clear mountain spring here. In tiny Nelsonville, tucked away in the Hudson Highlands, you will find some of the best hiking trails in the entire state; the New York State Greenway Conference recently named Nelsonville the "Hiker's Hamlet."

This unique little corner of New York State, just out of reach of the Big Apple, is a wonderful welcome mat to the cool air, cozy surroundings, and country comforts of an area we call Upstate.

REFERENCE FILE

Sybil Ludington has seemingly been "discovered" just over the past couple of decades or so. There are now countless books and articles written about her. One of the best is *Sybil Ludington: The Call to Arms* by V. T. Dacquino (Purple

Mountain Press, 2000). For history about Ludington's famous connection to the region, visit http://www.danburymuseum.org/.

With the exception of Rodin (the Crown Point Lighthouse) and Gutzon Borglum (the Dr. Trudeau monument), no other sculptor included in the making of the monuments in this book was as famous as Anna Hyatt Huntington. This towering figure on the art scene is considered to be among the finest sculptors this country has ever produced. Huntington (from nearby Bethel, Connecticut) presented this statue to the Enoch Crosby Chapter of the Daughters of the American Revolution of Carmel in 1961. (Enoch Crosby was the Revolutionary War hero who had given Sybil the horse she rode on her famous journey.) For more about this famous sculptor, including photographs of her many works, visit http://www .brookgreen.org.

14

"I WILL FACE THE ENEMY!"

The General Herkimer Monument, Herkimer

THE PLACE

Herkimer, New York, is centrally located in the state at Exit 30 off the New York State Thruway, the halfway point between Albany and Syracuse. To the north, the village crawls up to the foothills of the Adirondack Mountains, and to the south, the Mohawk River cuts through it as a natural boundary.

The village holds about 8,000 residents and has an amazing array of historical points of interest within its five square miles. Herkimer, named for Revolutionary War hero General Nicholas Herkimer, was an early home to Palatine Germans and Native Americans, and with few exceptions, these diverse groups lived in relative harmony for generations. When the Germans arrived in about 1720, the Mohawks had already been here for more than a hundred years in their village named Indian Castle. During the Revolutionary War period, the village on the other side of the river was called Palatine, and later German Flatts (with a nod to its newest settlers).

The peaceful coexistence between the Indians and the Germanic settlers came to an abrupt end during the French and Indian War. In 1758, a village on the south of the river (now the town of Mohawk) was attacked, and thirty settlers were massacred. General Nicholas Herkimer commanded the fort in the village. It would not be the first skirmish this larger-than-life figure would be involved in.

The village of Herkimer is unique in that it answers to the laws of three different like-named governments: the village of Herkimer in the town of Herkimer in the county of Herkimer! Today the village buzzes with foot traffic, wide busy avenues, a plethora of pubs and cafés, youth-trendy shops (Herkimer County Community College and its 3,500 students are located here), and restaurants

of varying tastes. It is the county seat, and the county government is a major employer in the community. The 140-mile-long Mohawk River, which flows east across the southern edge of the village, is the largest tributary of the Hudson River and is the focal point for Herkimer's historic connection to the Erie Canal (a working lock is right at the southern doorstep to the village).

The entire region around the village of Herkimer is steeped in early American history, but the destiny of the man and the place named Herkimer was forged in the nearby Battle of Oriskany on August 6, 1777, dubbed the Bloodiest Day of the Revolutionary War.

THE MONUMENT

With nearby Fort Stanwix under siege by the British, General Nicholas Herkimer mustered up a force of about eight hundred men (the Tryon Militia at Fort Dayton, which was located in what is now downtown Herkimer) and marched on the fort, pulling some four hundred oxcarts of supplies along behind them, about thirty-five miles to the west. Herkimer's army was made up of poorly trained, ill–equipped, and unskilled farmers and villagers from the surrounding Germanic farm country as well as Dutch and English settlers. With the siege of Fort Stanwix stagnating to a tortuous standoff, the fort's commander, Col. Peter Gansevoort, desperately hoped for the quick arrival of new troops and arms, no matter what condition they were in.

The British commander of the siege of Fort Stanwix, Lt. Col. Barry St. Leger, caught wind of Herkimer's advance and sent forth a force of four hundred Mohawks, under Chief Joseph Brant, and two hundred loyalist soldiers, under Sir John Johnson, to intercept the advancing patriot militia. Their rendezvous with destiny would take place at a leafy ravine, which was crossed by a bubbling clear-water stream just a mere six miles from Herkimer's destination, Fort Stanwix. The calm of the day in this bucolic Eden would be shattered on the afternoon of August 6, 1777, when, in the course of a few short hours, massive casualties would litter the ground, clouds of heavy musket smoke would thicken the air, and the creek would run red with blood.

Herkimer's men, after a tough slog through raw wilderness, came upon this refreshing ravine and were eager to advance into it and to find respite from the dankness of a muggy August morning. The general, savvy in the wiles of combat, thought the place was a perfect spot for an ambush and hesitated to send his men forward. They waited. And they waited. Finally, tempted by the sounds of the cold fast-running stream and at the verge of mutiny, the men waded into the ravine with (although some historians think without) their leader's blessing. Some of the militiamen threw down their rifles and rejoiced at their good fortune of having arrived at a refreshing oasis.

Sensing a moment of surprise was at hand, the trap was sprung. General Herkimer had been right. Just hours before the arrival of his troops to this place, Chief Brant and Sir Johnson had arrived at the ravine, and they too knew that this locale presented a perfect place for an ambush. Johnson placed fifty of his best rifleman at the end of the ravine (to prevent an escape), and the Indian chief hid four hundred of his finest Mohawk warriors in the underbrush on both sides of the stream.

At the patriots' most vulnerable moment, the signal to attack was given. The crack of rifle fire and the war whoops of the attacking Mohawks must have frozen Herkimer and his troops with fear. A mighty battle raged immediately. With one of the first shots fired, General Herkimer's horse was shot out from under him. This same musket ball nearly severed his leg. Bleeding profusely, he ordered his men to drag him to a giant beech tree, where he was propped up against his saddle and continued to direct the battle. His junior officers pleaded with him to evacuate the battlefield. "I will face the enemy," he bellowed. He even lit one of his trademark long-stemmed clay pipes and puffed away as the maelstrom raged about him. The hand-to-hand combat was fierce, sometimes pitting neighbor against neighbor. Within one hour the creek was running a dark red from the spilled blood.

The battle was subdued by a well-timed thunderstorm, which gave the Americans a chance to regroup and rearm. Later that day, the fight was rejoined, and Herkimer's troops prevailed as Brant, Johnson, and what was left of their army left the battlefield staggered by their losses and the ferocity of the encounter. More than five hundred deaths took place in this famous ravine in the course of a few short hours. Because of its location, it is referred to in the history books today as the Battle of Oriskany, but many Upstaters know that terrible day as the Battle of Bloody Creek. It was the deadliest afternoon of the Revolutionary War.

Herkimer, in a dire condition, was strapped to a log raft and floated down the Mohawk River to his home, where a rushed amputation of his damaged leg took place. Infection set in and ten days later he was dead. At the moment of his death, he was seen propped up in his bed at his home, reading the Bible aloud and puffing on his famous pipe. He was forty-nine years old.

The General Herkimer Monument is a proud and muscular tribute to the hero this town is named after. Reaching twelve feet tall, the depiction shows the general in his position beneath the battlefield beech tree. You can see his wounded leg (unbooted and wrapped in bandages), you can see the pain etched in his face, you can see his magnificent officer's saddle, you can see his long-stemmed pipe and, yes, you can almost see the surrounding trees shudder with the crack of the patriot rifles, almost hear the blood-curdling yells of the Mohawk ambushers, and almost smell the pungent gunpowder as it singes your nose. It is that realistic!

Burr Miller, the sculptor son of former New York Senator Warren Miller, designed the statue. The monument sits atop an enormous boulder that was dragged by train and oxcart down from the Old Forge, New York, area to act as a base for the sculpture. It was dedicated with much fanfare in 1907.

To reach this grand memorial, enter the village of Herkimer from the south on the main road (State Street) and make a left at Prospect Street. After a couple of blocks you will come to Park Street; make a left and the street dead ends at the Herkimer Monument (which, curiously, bears a big scrawled signature of the German spelling of his name, "Hercheimer"). The park is known as Myers Park.

WHILE HERE

Herkimer's Historic Four Corners, at Main and Park streets, is a perfect place to begin your visit to this beautiful Upstate village. In fact, there is an afternoon's worth of "historic spelunking" right at these four corners. Fort Dayton was located here, marking the starting point of Gen. Herkimer's fateful march to Oriskany. One corner is anchored by the excellent Herkimer County Historical Museum, in the regal Suiter Mansion, built for a prominent physician in 1884. The staff here is quite knowledgeable and extremely friendly to those seeking information about Nicholas Herkimer and the community at large. The 1873 Herkimer County Courthouse, now used for the sheriff's office, anchors another corner. This grand Victorian building is a wonderful snapshot of the glory of 1800s Herkimer. It is a landmark and one of Herkimer's most beautiful buildings. In 1906, the Chester Gillette murder trial was held here, and news reporters from around the world flocked here to witness Gillette's conviction for the murder of his ex-girlfriend Grace Brown. Theodore Dreiser turned this real-life event into his popular 1925 novel *An American Tragedy*, which *Time* magazine named as one of the top 100 English-language novels of the twentieth century.

A third corner of these four historic parcels is home to the 1834 Reformed Church. Inside the church are breathtaking original Tiffany stained-glass windows, and outside, all around the exterior walls, are the gravestones of some of the region's earliest pioneers.

The churchyard burial ground was once a typical sight in Upstate New York, and the stones here are in remarkable condition to read and decipher.

The final (and I think most interesting) corner is the amazing Federal-style, fully restored 1834 Herkimer County Jail. Tours are given by well-versed docents from the Herkimer Historical Society, and exhibits inside include General Herkimer's battlefield sword and the Herkimer family Bible he was reading when he drew his last breath.

Two of the most sensational trials in the history of Upstate New York took place in Herkimer. The Gillette/Brown murder trial brought national, if not international, fame to this small rural community as what was then the crime of the century played out here. But it is the trial of the evil Roxalana Druse that still causes one to lose a good night's sleep.

Druse, of nearby rural Warren, New York, murdered her older husband (some say after years of abuse toward her) in the most cold-blooded of ways. She beat him senseless at his own dinner table, shot him through the back of his head, tied him to his dining room chair, forced (at the threat of their *own* deaths) her young children to shoot into his body, chopped him up with a chicken ax, boiled his dismembered body parts on her kitchen stove, and threw the results into the pigsty, where her porcine accomplices then ate the evidence. Clearly, this was a woman with a plan that she felt was foolproof!

Well, eventually the children gave up dear old Mom when authorities came snooping around looking for the long-missing Mr. Druse. Roxalana was tried and convicted of murder at the Herkimer County Courthouse and then was walked across the street to the jail, where she was hanged. Roxalana Druse is known as much in these parts for her execution as she is for her heinous crime. On February 28, 1887, she was walked out of the top, third-story door at the back of the jail, a noose was strung around her neck, and the trapdoor she was standing on was tripped.

The tiny hooded woman thrashed about like a worm trying to wriggle off a hook for more than *fifteen minutes* before her limp body signaled that she was dead. This botched hanging, which made many in the large crowd below sick to their stomachs, created as much of a furor as did the facts of her crime. Shortly thereafter, on June 4, 1888, death by hanging was outlawed in the state of New York, and the next execution (William Kemmler, August 6, 1890) was the first to be carried out by the new, official method of applying the death penalty, the electric chair. Poor Roxalana Druse was the last person in New York State history to be executed by hanging.

If you walk around to the back of the restored Herkimer County jail today, you can still look up and see the door she walked out of that freezing February day in 1887, and you can still see the steel hook above the door that held the hangman's noose.

One other sculptural note of interest in this area of Herkimer is a second statue to be found in Myers Park, just a few hundred feet from the great General Nicholas Herkimer Monument. It is a grand tribute to a famous resident of the village, someone of obvious importance, a more-than-life-size bronze figure of a handsome, older man in a fedora hat, with one hand tucked inside his expensive overcoat, his other hand resting firmly on a book (Bible?). But who is it? It was a mystery to me.

I walked around the towering statue, admiring the definition of the sculptor's work. I was intrigued by the inscription ("The fact that I was instrumental in introducing women to employment in the offices of the government gives me more real satisfaction than all the other deeds of my life"), and I recorded the name of the sculptor (H. J. Ellicott). I even tried to spell out the honored person's signature, which is grandly scrawled across the face of the monument. But to no avail. Off to the Herkimer Historical Society I went.

The mystery was solved with the help of the hospitable volunteers who delved into their card catalogs and microfiche to answer the riddle of the Mystery Man of Myers Park. And what a story it turned out to be. His name is Gen. Francis E. Spinner (1802–1890). The statue was dedicated in the park in 1894, and he was as close to a Renaissance man as Herkimer would ever produce. He was a sheriff, soldier, banker, draftsman, architect (he designed the historic jail from which Druse's neck was stretched), congressman, land speculator, *and* Abraham Lincoln's Civil War secretary of the Treasury.

As our nation's tenth Treasury cabinet officer, Spinner was known as "the father of fractional currency" (bills that were smaller than usual so as to accommodate the limits of the Civil War). He introduced "greenbacks" to our national terminology (using green ink on military demand notes), and was, as his monument so succinctly explains, the first man who allowed women to be employed in a government office. Throughout his term of office as secretary of the Treasury, F. E. Spinner was known for his florid, graceful (yet unintelligible) signature, which appeared on all commonly used bank notes. It is this indecipherable lettering that adorns the great monument to him here in Herkimer.

It is puzzling that no other explanation of who this man was appears at his statue. One can imagine that the many park visitors who are drawn to this grandiose tribute examine it and leave, scratching their heads and saying, "Who was that?"

Several diamond mines are located nearby to Herkimer. Gems found there are called Herkimer diamonds and are actually faceted quartz crystals. These "diamonds" have points on both ends and are found in just a few locations around the world. The mines are popular tourist destinations, and several generations of visitors have spent part of their summers bent over an open pit, chipping away at the ground looking for their treasures. Two of the most popular mines are the Herkimer Diamond Mine (Herkimer) and the Ace of Diamonds Mine (Middleville).

REFERENCE FILE

A terrific book about the Revolutionary War battles in the Herkimer area, including General Herkimer's role in them, is *Liberty March: The Battle of Oriskany* by Allan D. Foote (North Country Books, 1999).

United States Senator Warner Miller, a longtime Herkimer leading figure, donated the $5,000 to have the General Herkimer statue sculpted by his son, Burr. The sculptor took the statue and displayed it to critical acclaim at the main art salon in Paris, France. He then returned the statue to the village of Herkimer, where it was positioned in Myers Park, and his father officially gave the statue to the community. Sen. Miller had a long and distinguished career and was a key personality in the growth and development of Herkimer and the surrounding area. His biography can be found at http://bioguide.congress.gov.

15

THE WHITE WOMAN OF THE GENESEE

The Mary Jemison Statue, Letchworth State Park

THE PLACE

The Mary Jemison Statue is located within Letchworth State Park, thirty-five miles south of Rochester and four miles south on Route 32 out of the center of Cuylerville, New York.

Letchworth, known as the "Grand Canyon of the East," is certainly one of the most astonishingly beautiful places on the East Coast. With the Genesee River pouring into it from the south, the centuries of erosion have created an amazing landscape of gorges, ravines, cliffs, and lush forests. More than sixty miles of hiking trails and a series of towering waterfalls that are among the highest in the nation (some more than one hundred feet tall) make this a paradise for those who love the outdoors. The park, which celebrated its centennial in 2006, is a major tourist destination for thousands of visitors each summer. Also in the park is the Mount Morris Dam, the largest dam in America east of the Mississippi. The dam, built in 1952, at a cost of $25 million, was the end result of devastating floods that routinely ravaged the Genesee River Valley for more than a century. There are gift shops, restaurants, and restrooms at the Visitor Center. While viewing this remarkable spectacle of engineering from one of the breathtaking sightseeing platforms, you can see great crowds of majestic hawks swoop below as they prowl for food along the canyon ridges and river basin.

The park is huge and covers more than twenty-two square miles of sumptuous terrain in Western New York. Four towns border it, and you will find entrances to the park at each community: Mount Morris, Portageville, Castile, and Perry. Many places covet the sobriquet "Grand Canyon of the East," but none can compare to Letchworth. A simple search will turn up Quechee Gorge (Vermont),

Ausable Chasm (New York), Linville Gorge Wilderness (North Carolina), and others as pretenders to the throne. But for pure rustic regalness and for the sheer panorama of nature's natural nobility, Letchworth is the once and forever queen of them all.

The park houses campsites, hiking trails, restaurants and inns, whitewater tubing and rafting, vistas, swimming, bike paths, hot air ballooning, and horseback riding. It also contains one grave!

The grave belongs to Mary Jemison, "the white woman of the Genesee."

THE STATUE

Mary Jemison was born at sea in 1743. Her Irish parents had boarded the ship *William and Mary* and set out for the New World with other Scotch Irish immigrants. Thomas and Jane Jemison made their way to the region of Philadelphia, which was then a distant rough and tumble outpost on the far western frontier of the not-yet christened America (their farmstead was near present-day Gettysburg). The French and Indian War was raging at the time, and the Jemison farm came under attack from a French and Shawnee war party in 1758. The family farm was burned, and the entire Jemison clan was captured and taken prisoner. They were forced to march to Pittsburgh (then called Fort Duquesne), a trail that took them through tangled forests and over rocky mountain ranges. Eventually the war party grew tired of escorting such a burdensome group and a decision was made to kill the family. Thomas, Jane, and all of their children except fifteen-year-old Mary were murdered and scalped before reaching their destination. Mary was sold to two Seneca Indians upon arrival at the fort.

Mary Jemison showed enormous fortitude and courage during her captivity, and while always mourning the death of her family (they had been killed in front of her), she also quickly recognized her untenable predicament and over time adapted to her new life as a squaw. She was given the name Dehgewanus (Two Voices Falling) and eventually married a member of the Delaware tribe, a brave named Sheninjee. She bore him a son, whom she named Thomas in honor of her beloved father.

As the French and Indian War came to an end, Sheninjee believed that a peace treaty would require all Indians to return any captive whites, thereby forcing him to give up his loving young wife (something even Mary did not want to see happen). It is then that the Indian and his "white woman" began a truly remarkable odyssey. They walked for weeks, much of it through unmapped territory, from southern Pennsylvania north to an area of western New York where his ancestors had lived. The journey was more than 700 miles, and Mary did it all with little Thomas strapped to her back. Both mother and child reached the Indian camp safely; Sheninjee died while hunting for food for his wife and son along the route. Mary's heroic achievement was met with great awe and praise from her new family.

Eventually, Mary settled at Little Beard's Town (a Seneca capital located just outside of present-day Geneseo), married a Seneca named Hiakatoo, and bore him six children. When the Clinton-Sullivan Campaign laid waste to the Indian frontier in the late 1700s, Mary's homestead was left untouched. She lived as a revered member of the Seneca Nation until she died at the age of ninety on September 19, 1833. Dressed in a buckskin outfit and moccasins and accompanied by a bowl and spoon to nourish her along her spiritual journey, "the white woman of the Genesee" was buried in the Mission Burial Ground of the Buffalo Creek Reservation in Buffalo.

In her eightieth year, Mary was interviewed for a book on her life by author James Seaver. This interview, conducted at a tavern near Castile, offers the most accurate first person account of the incredible life of this unique woman. *A Narrative of the Life and Times of Mrs. Mary Jemison* sold more than 100,000 copies in its first year of publication.

Her journey into the afterlife would turn out to be as restless as the wandering years of her youth.

In 1871, her burial ground stood in the way of the robust expansion of Buffalo, then one of the nation's largest and most important cities. Vandals had chipped away at her original grave marker, the cemetery was in disrepair, and the city was about to turn it under.

Mary's grandchildren pleaded with millionaire businessman William Pryor Letchworth (1823–1910) to rebury their grandmother in the dignity she deserved at the Indian Council Grounds on his one-thousand-acre property (now Letchworth State Park). He readily agreed, having always been fascinated with Mary's story. Mary's grandson Dr. James Shongo supervised the exhumation of his famous relative. Mary's bones were placed in a black walnut coffin with silver adornments and placed aboard the Erie Railroad in Buffalo. In Castile, along the banks of the Genesee River, she was received with solemn pomp and circumstance. A large cortege trailed behind the wagon bearing the coffin to the Council Ground above Mr. Letchworth's home. There it was placed in a cement sarcophagus. At the end of the burial ritual, grandson Shongo, who had made the long final journey with his grandmother, opened the coffin and removed a piece of Mary's white hair as a remembrance of her. The coffin was then closed and cemented into the sarcophagus and buried. The date was March 7, 1874.

Letchworth State Park eventually enveloped Mary's grave, and today her final resting place is under the custodial care of park rangers. A stunningly magnificent life-sized statue of her stands behind a wrought iron fence delineating her grave. A new marker tells her tale (the old and chipped original marker can be seen nearby at the park museum). The inscription reads:

To the memory of MARY JEMISON. Whose home during more than seventy years of a life of vicissitude was among the Senecas upon the banks of this river; and whose history is now inseparably connected to this valley and has caused her to be known as "The White Woman of the Genesee." The remains of the

"White Woman" were removed from the Buffalo Creek Reservation and reinterred at this place with appropriate ceremonies on the 7th day of March, 1874.

The statue distinctly portrays the brave young woman perhaps in mid-jour-
ney between the Ohio and the Genesee valleys. She is dressed in typical Indian
garb, with animal skin leggings and a fringed skirt on, and her little baby Thomas
is strapped to a bulky baby board on her back. Mary's Irish features contrast with
her Indian outfit and long, braided hair. The name "Dehgewanus" is inscribed
across the front of the marble base.

The sculptor, Henry Kirke Bush-Brown (1857–1935), was one of the foremost
depicters of Americana of the 1800s. Born in Ogdensburg, he is most famous for
his powerful busts and statues dotting the landscape of the Gettysburg battlefield.
His heroic tributes to Generals Meade, Sedgwick, Reynolds, and Sheridan are
diminished only by his famous bust of President Abraham Lincoln at the Gettysburg Address Memorial at the entrance to the National Cemetery there. The
bust, dedicated on January 22, 1912, has been called one of the most realistic
interpretations of the president ever cast. The bust is flanked by the words of the
Gettysburg Address (note that this is not at the actual site of Lincoln's speech, but
at the entrance to the cemetery).

The Mary Jemison statue underwent a complete refurbishing in 2006 to celebrate the centennial of the park.

WHILE HERE

To fully experience the grandeur of this park, a two-day visit should be scheduled.
To name just a few of the site's highlights does injustice to this incredible place. The
park ($8.00 entrance fee) includes the above-mentioned Mount Morris Dam, worth
a trip here all by itself. Other highlights include the Portage Wooden Bridge (also
known as the High Bridge), the only opportunity to cross the gorge from one side
to the other. The bridge offers breathtaking views from above of the Grand Canyon
of the East, and it is the highest and longest wooden railroad bridge in the world.

Note: One of the most frequently ignored signs in the park is the "No Tres-
passing" sign at the entrance to the bridge. Still used by an occasional train, the
track beds are usually peopled with tourists and hikers alike enjoying a truly "once
in a lifetime" experience, albeit an illegal one!

Inspiration Point offers the most glorious view in the park. The panorama includes towering pine trees, gouged rock gorges, and mist-spraying waterfalls. The waterfalls are periodically lit up at night for the enjoyment of park visitors. This point is located less than one mile from the Mount Morris entrance to the park. Another interesting historical fact in the park is the existence of St. Helena, the Ghost Town of Letchworth. A visitor's map can be followed to the site where once the flourishing town of St. Helena stood, with more than a hundred citizens, a school, mills, churches, and even a cemetery. Bad luck and an unruly Genesee River eventually erased all until the town completely vanished in 1954.

The Glen Iris Inn is located near Mary Jemison's grave. This grand mansion, now a popular inn and restaurant, was once the splendid home of William Pryor Letchworth and is immaculately restored to its original 1860 glory (http://www .glenirisinn.com). It is located right at the thunderous Middle Falls, which are best viewed from the inn. Sixteen rooms welcome visitors for an overnight stay at the exact spot that Letchworth picked out while traveling on a train over the Portage Wooden Bridge in the spring of 1858. He had taken that trip to clear his mind and ease his nerves from the pressures of big city business. He was on a journey to find a place where he could decompress from his business and financial constrictions and focus more on relaxation, communing with nature, enjoying fine prose and art, and welcoming family and guests to a Shangri-La in the woods. From the High Bridge he spied a run down house on a couple of hundred acres. He met the desperate owner, Michael Smith, a man on the brink of bankruptcy. He knew he had found his new sanctuary. A handshake later, William Pryor Letchworth was the new owner of two hundred acres and the place where his future Glen Iris estate would be built.

Letchworth paid Theodore Olcott (Smith's mortgage holder) $7,000 for the house and property. Smith received $1.00. Letchworth first slept at his future home, which he named after Iris, the goddess of rainbows, on July 4, 1859.

He bequeathed his thousand-acre estate to the state in 1906, forming the heart of the now fifteen-thousand-acre state park.

REFERENCE FILE

Bush-Brown had been a prolific designer of many Civil War monuments, and he looked at the Mary Jemison commission as a needed break from the stiff depictions of soldiers in uniform. He threw himself into the Jemison statue. He searched for local girls to pose for him and researched authentic native outfits that would have been worn by Jemison. He did exhaustive studies on human movement so as to correctly depict the heroine in motion. This story and more can be found at the Web site http://www.letchworthparkhistory.com.

The Letchworth Guidebook by William C. Greene (Vanmark Printing, 1981) is a good companion when visiting the park.

THE OLIVE TREE BY THE LAKE

The Deir Yassin Massacre Memorial, Geneva

Most states have a "hidden" region that may not be the most familiar to summer tourists, but rather remains a well-guarded "secret" area to be enjoyed and preserved by the locals of the region.

In California, thousands of tourists swarm Hollywood and San Francisco every summer, but far sparser crowds explore the high desert areas or the thinly populated regions of the California/Oregon border (both areas are fascinating but as far from "typical California" as you can get). In Texas, the cities of Houston, San Antonio, and Dallas teem in the summer with millions of residents and visitors, while the crowds in the Germanic Texas Hill Country, with its country fairs, wurstfests, and relaxing tubing adventures along the Guadalupe River enjoy about as different a Texas tradition as you can find in the Lone Star State.

In Pennsylvania, folks by the thousands cram the steamy streets of Philadelphia each summer, standing in line to take a snapshot of the Liberty Bell or Ben Franklin's grave, but more savvy visitors explore the cooler confines of Wyeth's pastoral Delaware Water Gap region or the nostalgic far western Pocono Mountain honeymoon retreats. In the summer in South Carolina, it is wall-to-wall skin at the beaches of Charleston, Hilton Head, and Myrtle Beach, but more adventurous tourists will find respite in the slower pace of the "Saratoga of the South" (Aiken) or the Appalachian Mountain lakes of the western part of the state. Massachusetts has its Berkshires, Florida has its "other" (west) coast, Tennessee has its horse country, Vermont has its Northeast Kingdom, and so on.

In the Empire State, many Upstaters would be happy if the bulk of the millions who visit New York each year would satisfy themselves with a Broadway

show, a salute to Lady Liberty, a Nathan's hot dog at Coney Island, or a Yankee game at the "house that Ruth built." For in far Western New York, there is a region of such rare beauty and of such treasured natural bounty that they would love to keep it a secret for as long as possible.

Welcome to the Finger Lakes.

Formed during the prehistoric glacial age, the eleven lakes defined as the Finger Lakes are resplendent with crystal waters, lush hills, quaint villages and small cities, fascinating indigenous arts and crafts, centuries of important American history, and folktales enough to keep a teenaged camper up all night around a campfire. And wineries!

Bearing the Indian names of (east to west) Otisco, Skaneateles, Owasco, Cayuga, Seneca, Keuka, Canandaigua, Honeoye, Canadice, Hemlock, and Coneseus, the Finger Lakes parade out just a few miles from each other along a band between (approximately) the large cities of Syracuse and Buffalo and directly below the second most populated city in Upstate New York, Rochester. The communities along the Finger Lakes Trail make good use of their lakeside attributes. New Englandy in style and ambiance, they adhere to the shores of their meal tickets with fierce pride. Some of the larger cities of the Finger Lakes region are found anchoring the southern end of the lakes. Ithaca, for example, with more than 30,000 citizens, is the largest Finger Lakes community and hugs the base of Cayuga Lake. But it is along the northern Finger Lakes Trail that the region really beckons the discerning roamer.

From Cazenovia in the east (although most consider Cazenovia Lake a "cousin" to the others in the lake chain) to Canandaigua in the west, the trip along the northern tips of the lakes is wondrous. And the history you will find in this "secret area" of the state is amazing. Seneca Falls is the birthplace of the women's rights movement; Waterloo is the birthplace of Memorial Day; Auburn is the birthplace of Old Sparky (William Kemmler was the first person to die in the electric chair at the state penitentiary here on August 6, 1890); Hammond-sport is the "cradle of aviation" (Glenn Curtiss, a native here, was a rival of the Wright Brothers and held US Pilot's License no. 1); and Watkins Glen was the home of the American Grand Prix for more than two decades and is still a popular stop on the Nascar race tour.

The trail follows closely the Erie Canal, at the time of its building a great engineering marvel and a key to our country's expansion in the nineteenth century. Many stretches of the canal are used today for pleasure craft and other public uses. A large number of the historic locks, which were constructed under unbelievably horrible conditions by thousands of immigrant workers, still stand as mute testimony to the courage displayed and hardships endured during the building of Clinton's ditch.

And all along this historic journey across New York, you can be refreshed at more than two dozen nationally ranked wineries (New York State ranks third in US wine production).

One of the most beautiful of the historic lake communities in the Finger Lakes is Geneva. With a population of fewer than 15,000, Geneva sits hard on the northwestern rim of Seneca Lake. It makes excellent use of the stunning lakefront, with homes, businesses, and public areas all claiming precious lake rights in an unfettered atmosphere. Called the lake trout capital of the world, Geneva arguably has more lake activity than any of the other above-mentioned communities. The city plays host to two thousand students each year at Hobart and William Smith Colleges. Elizabeth Blackwell graduated here on January 24, 1849, at the top of her class as the first woman doctor in America. Some say the city was named after its sister city in Switzerland because of its splendid natural beauty, although others admit that the name might be construed as to how the word "Seneca" looks when written in ancient cursive. In either case, there are no doubters that Geneva is one of the most stunning of New York's jewels, a destination that will richly reward the traveler with beauty, history, and adventure.

It is unsettling then that Geneva is included in this book because of the monument located here.

It is a monument to a massacre.

THE MEMORIAL

Of all the monuments in this book, this memorial is the most difficult (but not impossible) to find. The hunt for the Deir Yassin Remembered (DYR) marker leads the traveler to an emotional touchstone to the past that symbolizes the anguish and torment felt by Arab Americans and Palestinians everywhere over events that happened more than sixty years ago.

In April 1948, the Arab-Israeli wars of larger proportions were still years away, but skirmishes, terrorist raids, and fast ranging battles were commonplace throughout the Middle East. The year before, the United Nations had decreed a separated Palestine: Jewish and Arab. The act (UN Resolution 181) also internationalized Jerusalem. Tensions were high in the region, and insurgent groups on both sides grew bolder and bolder as borders began to shift and populations went on the move. A battle of the roads began, as supply convoys and tides of refugees began to be a supple target for terrorists on both sides. Arab forces, in particular, began a concentrated effort to sever the main highway and bloodline between the major Jewish cities of Tel Aviv and Jerusalem. This attempt at a siege of Jerusalem meant the Arab towns in the mountains overlooking the road in and out of the city became prize possessions. The village of Deir Yassin occupied an aerie above the road, making it a perfect location for an Israeli takeover and for the future location of a new military airstrip.

What happened between April 9 and April 11, 1948, has been debated between the two warring sides for more than a half-century. The facts are that the Israeli forces entered the town, many civilians died in the military attack, the Jewish forces (including the militant army Irgun, headed by future Israeli prime minister Menachem Begin) occupied the village, a series of Arab retaliatory raids enflamed the situation, and the Arab-Israeli wars of the next several generations became predestined. What is not clear are the number of civilian casualties (the range swings wildly from ninety to seven hundred) and the breadth of the atrocities committed. Some cite mass murders in the street, others suggest torture and drownings, and still others claim Israeli self-defense to well-dug-in defenders. Arabs consider the event at Deir Yassin a massacre. The Israelis do not.

It is by no means the intent of this entry in *Monumental New York!* to explain, analyze, defend, or oppose the politics or historic interpretations of what happened in this small faraway village in 1948. Rather, it is the intent of this book to highlight an unusual, rare memorial to a tragic and dark event that ended up being erected in a stunningly peaceful, totally remote, pristinely quiet lakeside locale in an aptly named Upstate New York community known as Geneva.

First, a description of the monument itself. Then directions to its locale (the former is easy; the latter is not).

In the words of the memorial design committee itself: "The Geneva memorial is a bronze sculpture depicting a mature olive tree, a symbol of peace, uprooted in the quest to build a Jewish state on land owned and long-inhabited by Muslim and Christian Palestinians. The tree's tortured, angular lines illustrate the Palestinian dispossession that began in 1948 and continues today. The extended branches add movement and drama; they appear dead and yet are still alive. The torn roots of the displaced olive tree are partially wrenched from the earth; their continued attachment to the ground symbolizes clinging to the motherland."

The bronze monument, officially titled Memorial on the Lake: Deir Yassin Remembered, is on a granite base. The nearly six-foot-tall monument is beautifully crafted, and the olive tree is graceful and yet tortured. The sculptor, Khalil Bendib, is considered to be America's most successful Muslim Arab artist, with many pieces of public art on display around the country. He lives in Berkeley, California.

A haiku on the adorning plaque reads:

> Earth torn roots yearning
> Palestine landscape mourning
> Displaced descendants

The author is Randa Hamwi Duwaji, director of poetry for the DYR project. The plaque continues on with the historical litany of the Deir Yassin event.

The juxtaposition of the gnarled bronze tree branches, stretching out against the stiff lake breezes and searching, perhaps (or maybe just beckoning), against the picturesque backdrop of the clear blue placid waters of Seneca Lake is really a stirring and poignant tableau.

To find the DYR memorial, you must first find the Geneva on-the-Lake Resort. This storied Triple AAA Four Diamond rated resort is located just south of the Geneva city center at 1001 Lochland Drive (Route 14). The hotel was built as a private villa in 1914 and is constructed of Italian marble. Situated on a private ten-acre lakeside parcel, the resort holds one of the most beautiful locations in the Finger Lakes region. Lake views extend for miles, a maze of Versailles-like gardens decorate the ten-acre back lawn, giant statues add a distinctly Roman feeling, and a seventy-foot marble swimming pool sits high above Seneca Lake. It is a favorite for romantic getaways, corporate parties, and weddings (*Bride* magazine has called the resort "one of the world's most beautiful inns"). It is on the National Registry of Historic Places.

In 1995, Alfred and Aminy Audi purchased the historic Geneva-on-the-Lake Resort. Their story is a classic tale of American success. In 1973 they sold their furniture business in New York City and bought the ailing and quickly vanishing Stickley Furniture Company. The Stickley line of furniture had once been a pioneer in Mission style furniture and the Arts and Crafts movement, and it was a booming business under the tutelage of founder Gustav Stickley and his brothers, John and Leopold. After their deaths (John in 1921, founder Gustav in 1942, and Leopold in 1957), the company fell into the hands of Leopold's widow, Louise, and from that point on the patina of success at Stickley Furniture began to fade.

Louise was a legendary curmudgeon with little business leadership experience or qualities. With a more modern and changing work force necessary, she refused to hire women in the furniture factory (or men with long hair). Needless to say, the ripple effect of her mismanagement was devastating, and soon, with only twenty employees and virtually no income, Louise called one of Stickley's last remaining dealers and offered the business up for sale. That business was Audi's Furniture. Alfred Audi and his wife Aminy closed the deal, relocated from Manhattan to rural Upstate New York (the Syracuse area), and began a business plan to turn the company around. And did they ever!

Today, the Stickley Company employs more than one thousand workers and racks up sales nearing $150 million annually. Sadly, Alfred died in 2007. The Audis were generous benefactors to many Upstate New York organizations as well as wealthy entrepreneurs. With their ethic of hard work and excellence, they created one of the most historic, popular, and successful inns in Upstate New York (and yes, all the rooms are stylishly decorated with Stickley furniture!).

Aminy Audi, a native of Lebanon, has been a generous supporter of the DYR project since its inception. It is here, at her lakeside Upstate New York resort, that the monument was finally erected. She was a key fundraiser for the memorial.

To reach "the olive tree by the lake," park in the circular driveway in front of the resort. As you are looking at the front facade, walk around to the left side of the building (the northern edge) and proceed to the sweeping back yard. Staying to the left fringe of the property, continue toward the lake and eventually a worn path through the trees will lead you down the steep bluff to the lakefront. Don't be alarmed when, at the bottom of the bluff, you come upon a pair of railroad tracks. Cross over the track (carefully look both ways; there is no crossing warning here) and on your left you will see a dock jutting out into the water. Before that is a tree-shaded minipark positioned right at the water's edge. A large semicircular marble bench invites one to sit and reflect on the DYR memorial, which is now directly in front of you.

Note: The trek to this out-of-the-way location is adventuresome but not arduous if you proceed with caution. The elderly or handicapped are advised to visit the DYR memorial with assistance.

WHILE HERE

Although the city of Geneva and the surrounding area are rich in history, studded with tasty wineries, and convenient for all types of shopping (from handicrafts to outlet shopping), my best suggestion would be to time your visit to the DYR memorial with a planned stay at the resort. Teas, Sunday brunches, formal dinners, cocktails on the back lawn, a pontoon boat ride on the lake, and more would all add a memorable touch to a visit to the unforgettable Geneva-on-the-Lake Resort and a visit to this, the hardest monument in this book to find. The hotel's Web site is http://www.genevaonthelake.com.

An excellent book on Deir Yassin is *Remembering Deir Yassin: The Future of Israel and Palestine* by Daniel McGowan (Interlink Publishing Group, 1998). A rare book about Geneva's past is well worth seeking out. It is titled *An Elegant but Salubrious Village* by Warren Hunting Smith (Geneva Historical Society, 1931). Smith's family helped found Hobart and William Smith Colleges in Geneva. When the Audi family purchased the Stickley Furniture Company, they were acquiring one of the great names in American design. For information on Gustav Stickley and his life and times, an excellent reference is *The Furniture of Gustav Stickley: History, Techniques and Projects* by Joseph Bavaro (Linden Publishing, 1997).

For a look at the works of artist Khalil Bendib (covering his pieces in oils, bronze, ceramics and mosaics), visit his Web site at http://www.studiobendib .com. The site includes photographs of the Memorial on the Lake: Deir Yassin Remembered.

17

GUNS FOR GENERAL WASHINGTON

The Knox Cannon Trail Monuments

The Knox Cannon Trail traverses more than three hundred miles, from Fort Ticonderoga, in far northern New York State, along a southeasterly route to just outside of Boston. The route meanders through mostly rural Upstate New York and follows the journey of Henry Knox, a Boston bookseller, friend of Washington, and future hero of the Revolutionary War. A rotund master planner, he pulled off one of the greatest feats in American military history. The Knox Cannon Trail consists of fifty-six identical monuments (thirty of them in New York State) following the path of this Herculean accomplishment. No other state has such a tribute, and the Knox Cannon Trail (originally commemorated in 1926, the 150th anniversary of the actual event) has been called America's first heritage trail.

The route goes through the heart of Revolutionary War New York. From historic Fort Ticonderoga south through the villages and towns of Lake George, Hudson Falls, Fort Edward, Saratoga, Mechanicville, the city of Albany, across the Hudson River and on to Rensselaer, Schodack, Kinderhook, Claverack, and into Massachusetts, the path is a virtual history primer of our nation's fight for independence. The region was the center of much of New York's participation in the war, and great battles (Saratoga), great generals (Philip Schuyler), and great events (the murder of Jane McCrea) all took place in the area of this trail.

What exactly did Henry Knox do? Experts today have called it, simply, beyond belief. General George Washington's army had the British nearly surrounded in Boston in the winter of 1775, nearly because Washington could not close the back door on his siege of the city. That back door was the vital harbor of Boston, which remained firmly in British hands. Because of this, weapons and

supplies were brought into the British army routinely, while the colonists could do little more than watch. Washington knew the key to completing the siege was to control the heights around the city, in Dorchester. Still, he lacked any large cannon to employ on these heights, where they could rain down fire on General Howe and his British army and force them to leave. Henry Knox had an idea.

The newly fallen Fort Ticonderoga, in northern New York, was in friendly hands and clearly without fear of another British takeover. The ramparts of the sturdy fort were lined with powerful artillery, now staring silently over Lake Champlain (Ethan Allan, Benedict Arnold, and a band of eighty-three Green Mountain Boys had captured the hulking fort from the British without firing a shot on May 10, 1775). Knox wanted to go and retrieve those cannon and bring them to Boston for Washington. Several highest ranking officers thought the plan foolish, but Washington did not, and he agreed to let the twenty-five-year-old Knox muster up a small party and get the much needed weaponry.

Over the next three months, Knox's accomplishments were incredible. He liberated fifty-six large cannons (sixty tons of armament) and dragged, sledded, floated, pushed, and urged them and his teams of oxen, homemade wagons, and river barges along the primitive wilderness route. The weather was horrible; the river froze, thawed, and then refroze; snowdrifts "higher than a man" blocked roads; and uncharted wilderness routes were a bothersome hindrance. Still, Knox conquered the elements and the sheer physical obstacles of his mission and soldiered on for a grinding fifty-six days, until he arrived in Dorchester with fifty-five cannon. He lost one when the Hudson River thawed while he was crossing it, but he did not lose a single man. Under the cover of darkness, Washington positioned the cannon atop the heights and supplemented his newfound firepower with painted logs to make the armament seem even more overwhelming.

At daybreak, General Howe spied the cannon barrels looking down at him and said, "The rebels have done more in one night than my army could do in one month!" Within hours he was retreating to Canada, and Boston was once again a free city.

General Henry Knox is one of the most interesting military men in our nation's history. And one of the most important. He was one of Washington's closest advisors and under his patronage rose through the ranks to the highest levels. He organized the general's Christmas crossing of the Delaware River and supervised the return trip, with Washington, his men, more than two thousand enemy prisoners, tons of British arms and supplies, and every boat that was afloat along the river (so as to truncate a British retaliation). For his actions, Washington made Knox a brigadier general.

Knox built (with limited means) sturdy life-saving forts at Valley Forge, and after witnessing the surrender of Cornwallis at Yorktown, he was commissioned a major general. When Washington said farewell to his troops on December 4, 1783, at Fraunces Tavern in New York City, Knox was at his side.

Knox was named our country's first secretary of war and retired in 1794 to his country manor, Montpelier, in Maine. The three-hundred-pound war hero died suddenly after ingesting a chicken bone in 1806.

The US gold depository, Fort Knox, and the city of Knoxville, Tennessee, are both named in his honor.

THE MONUMENTS

Each of the expedition's monuments (thirty in New York and twenty-six in Massachusetts) is identical in content. All consist of a large six-foot-tall granite boulder with a bronze bas-relief plaque affixed to the front (the only difference in the monuments in either state is the size of the plaque; the New York plaques are three times larger than the plaques in Massachusetts). The sculpture on the plaque depicts General Knox spurring on his oxen train loaded with cannon. The weather conditions in the image closely reflect the harsh natural obstacles he had to face. Along the left side of the sculpture is a topographic map showing the cannon trail route. The text reads: "Through this place passed Gen. Henry Knox in the winter of 1775–1776 to deliver to Gen. George Washington at Cambridge the train of artillery from Fort Ticonderoga used to force the British Army to evacuate Boston."

Through the years, weather and age have taken their toll on a number of monuments, but others have been "adopted" by various groups and communities and seem in remarkable shape. A 1926 New York State Commission laid out plans for the design and placement of these monuments.

Compared to other historic monuments, the Knox Cannon Trail seems a little underwhelming upon first viewing, especially due to the fact that each monument is exactly alike. The heroic event these markers memorialize, however, is nothing short of unbelievable.

The Clinton-Sullivan Campaign of 1779, ordered by General Washington to "clean up the Indian problem" in Western New York and parts of Pennsylvania, is commemorated with a similar series of identical monuments spread along the historic route of the event. However, the fifty-five monuments of this 1779 campaign cover hundreds of miles and would be extremely difficult to follow in one comprehensive trip.

WHILE HERE

The three-hundred-mile-long trail of monuments will take you through some of New York's most beautiful territory. It is not difficult to actually follow the Knox Cannon Trail (maps of the monument locations can be found at Fort

Ticonderoga as well as online at http://www.hudsonrivervalley.org). Also, there are three "must see" stops along the trail that will enrich, inform, and enhance your visit to upstate New York.

Fort Ticonderoga (Lake Champlain) and Fort William Henry (Lake George Village) are two superb examples of Revolutionary-period forts and are very popular with tourists. Both offer a variety of exhibits and events annually. A third important stop is the crucial Saratoga battlefield, just south of Lake George. Guided tours are available at this National Historic Landmark, which is operated by the National Park Service.

The Knox Cannon Trail goes through Albany, the state capital and a city with much vibrancy and history. The trail also wends its way through some of New York's most picturesque communities.

The monuments are remarkably easy to find, although two of the fifty-six are missing, having fallen victim to time and changing population trends (and highway reconfiguration). Still, at easy-to-maneuver intervals, the trip along the trail is historic and beautiful, especially in the autumn.

NY Monument no. 1 is located right on the parade grounds of historic Fort Ticonderoga itself, Knox's starting point. Heading south, then east, you will find the next monument. Other easily seen monuments can be found at Rogers Memorial Park in Bolton, on the grounds of the Hudson Falls public library, on the front lawn of Fort Edward High School, at the village park in Schuylerville, in front of the Mechanicville post office, on a tiny piece of grass sandwiched between a shopping center and Albany Memorial Hospital, at the Reformed Church in East Greenbush, and near the President Van Buren statue in Kinderhook (featured in chapter 28). The thirtieth and final monument is located on Route 71 at the New York/Massachusetts state line. This one has text on both sides marking the end of the New York portion of the trail and the beginning of the Massachusetts segment.

REFERENCE FILE

There is no record of the artist who crafted the image, which is on each of the fifty-six monuments. An interesting Web site that details the monuments and the trail is http://www.hmdb.org (the Historical Marker Data Base site). Here you can also see a photograph of Tom Lovell's heroic painting *Noble Train of Artillery*, which is currently on display at Fort Ticonderoga.

An excellent book on the life of the much-unheralded General Knox is *Henry Knox: Visionary General of the American Revolution* by Mark Puls (Palgrave Macmillan, 2010).

LET'S HAVE TEA

The Anthony-Douglass Statue, Rochester

Upstate New York was in the forefront of the abolitionist movement, and Rochester was perhaps its most important city. Many of the great antislavery leaders made Rochester their home. Abolitionist newspapers were big sellers on the streets of the city, and the Underground Railroad was virtually "above ground" in this beacon of liberalism on the western New York plain.

Frederick Douglass, "the lion of abolition," produced his newspaper The *North Star* here in 1847 (the building still exists). It was the leading soapbox for antislavery voices of the time. Rochester, it has been said, has more verified locations of Underground Railroad safe houses than any other Upstate New York city. Susan B. Anthony, active in so many of the social causes of the period, was a longtime Rochester resident who drew a national spotlight to this city (her home is now a museum).

With a greater metropolitan area of around one million people, Rochester is New York's third most populated city (behind New York City and Buffalo). The city was the focal point for all central New York industry, trade, and transportation in the early 1800s. The Erie Canal went right through the heart of the city, and mills churned out many of the dry goods needed to settle the even farther western parts of the state. Between 1830 and 1840, Rochester's population doubled, from 10,000 to 20,000 residents, making the city the first certified boomtown of its era. Known as the Flour City, it ranked as the fourth largest flour producer in the world during this period.

Today Rochester is a high-tech center with Fortune 500 companies, nationally ranked universities, and sprawling medical centers. Wegmans Food Markets, a locally owned, nationally recognized supermarket chain, is headquartered in Rochester and carries a hefty payroll of nearly 5,000 workers. Wegmans takes pride in its seventy-plus stores and its thousands of employees. In 2007 the Food Network named it America's best supermarket, and in 2009 *Consumer Reports* named it the nation's number one grocery chain. It is currently the seventh largest food store in the United States.

Rochester is home to several great museums, including the Strong National Museum of Play (which houses the National Toy Hall of Fame) and the George Eastman House and Museum. George Eastman, the father of American photography, was a benefactor of great scope to his beloved Rochester. His fifty-room mansion (900 East Avenue) is intact as it was the day in 1932 when he died in the upstairs bedroom of a self-inflicted gunshot wound. The dining room table is set for guests, the music room is ready for a concert, and the well-stocked library is ready to welcome friends and family for a snifter of brandy. One of the most jaw-dropping features of the Eastman House is the reception area, where George would entertain with local musicians and singers. It boasts an enormous pipe organ, which is situated so as to echo throughout all corners of the thirty-thousand-square-foot home. A life-sized stuffed elephant, bagged on a safari, appears to be crashing through the walls above your head, ivory tusks and all!

The rear of the mansion is the location of the International Museum of Photography and Film. It has the largest and oldest film archive in the world. The museum actively undergoes the preservation of precious film works and hosts speakers and exhibits pertaining to photography and film.

There are many pleasant ways to spend a weekend in Rochester, especially during the annual Lilac Festival, when tens of thousands of the purple blossoms perfume the air. Also, there is much history to explore. And no matter what aspect you venture into, the canal, film, the railroads, or politics, it is virtually impossible to escape the long shadow cast by two American giants who lived and worked in Rochester at the same time, for many of the same reasons.

They are the legendary Susan B. Anthony and Frederick Douglass.

THE STATUE

"The mother of the women's rights movement," Susan B. Anthony spent her most politically active years at her home located at 17 Madison Street. That home is now a museum to her achievements as well as a wondrous look back to an era of gentility and Victorian charm. The house has many of Anthony's original belongings and furniture in it as well as displays and exhibits that change frequently (http://susanbanthonyhouse.org/index.php). Anthony lived here for years, was dramatically arrested here in 1872 for daring to vote in an election, and died here. The surrounding ten-block area features quaint homes and tree-lined streets, all preserved to reflect the era of Susan B. Anthony's residence here. A block from her home and museum is Susan B. Anthony Square. A pretty, well-manicured public space, it is crisscrossed by winding stone paths and is lit by old-fashioned street lamps. The square is a friendly and well-used public park for the neighborhood. At the very center of the park is a remarkable double statue.

Sculptor Pepsy M. Kettavong, a neighborhood resident, has positioned Susan B. Anthony and the great Frederick Douglass facing each other, sitting in sturdy yet comfortable-looking high-backed chairs, seemingly in deep conversation. On a small table between them is a teapot, teacups, and some books. Both are gesturing to the other. It is an unusual statue in that it depicts two major figures in American history in such a light, casual pose. Also, the fact that the statue was placed at ground level, without a base or pedestal, gives you the feeling that you are interrupting a couple of old friends who happen to be having a friendly cup of tea together in a small neighborhood park. Let's Have Tea instantly draws you into the scene, quiets your soul, and causes a smile to cross your lips, perhaps more so than any other memorial I observed in research for this book.

Kettavong, a Laotian American, dedicated the statue to the city of Rochester on August 26, 2001, exactly eighty-one years to the day that American women gained the right to vote. Various Rochester civic groups provided the $10,000 commission fee to the sculptor.

WHILE HERE

Rochester holds an embarrassment of riches for the weekend visitor. Without a doubt, time must be spent at the George Eastman House and Museum. There is literally something for everyone here (http://www.eastmanhouse.org). The home itself, built in 1905 and listed as a National Historic Landmark, is a maze of rooms (thirty-seven rooms and thirteen bathrooms), an eye-popping panorama of period furnishings and artifacts, and a treasure trove of local Rochester lore. The museum holds seventy-five thousand square feet of exhibition space housing more than four hundred thousand photographs. The museum gift shop is packed with curios, trinkets, and an array of high quality photography-themed souvenirs. The formal gardens surrounding the home are lush and gorgeous, and they are the scene of numerous weddings and parties, all at a flat access fee of $1,500 per event!

In many of the larger cities of New York (Albany, Buffalo, New York City), the main burying grounds are massive places consisting of thousands of graves, miles of roads and paths, dozens of lakes and ponds, and acres of trees, gardens, and plantings. Usually, these peaceful, beautiful garden spots are located near the heart of the old city. It seems odd that these "cities of the dead" are such welcoming places, but they are. Tourists by the hundreds visit the great cemeteries of New York City (such as Woodlawn and Green Wood) each weekend looking for the final resting places of the famous dead. Concertgoers, picnickers, and joggers keep Forest Lawn Cemetery in Buffalo a busy place every weekend; the cemetery is also the home of the only Frank Lloyd Wright–designed mausoleum in the world. Albany Rural Cemetery conducts weekend bicycle tours of the graveyard's sprawling five hundred acres, and here in Rochester, famous Mount Hope Cemetery is one of the top locales for visitors and history buffs alike.

The cemetery, a Victorian landmark in and of itself, holds more than 350,000 graves of the mighty and the unknown, all inside the two hundred acres of property located at 1133 Mount Hope Avenue, adjacent to the University of Rochester. Several different public tours are offered, such as those on Victorian sculpture, famous graves, Civil War, horticulture, and ghosts.

Both of the subjects of Let's Have Tea rest eternally at Mount Hope. Susan B. Anthony is buried in Section C, Lot 93. Frederick Douglass is in Section T, Lot 26. Maps to their graves are available at the cemetery office.

The Strong National Museum of Play (One Manhattan Square, downtown Rochester) recently underwent a $37 million renovation, nearly doubling in size. It holds a vast collection of exhibits of "everything play," from toys to books to interactive games to dolls. The founder of the museum, Margaret Woodbury Strong (1897–1969), a beloved Rochester philanthropist, had the world's largest private collection of dolls at the time of her death. The buildings are dramatically designed and colored and include a variety of eating venues to accommodate a full day's visit here. One of the eateries is a local favorite, Bill Gray's Skyliner Diner, a classic 1950s-era diner situated at the food court. The museum's Web site is http://www.museumofplay.org.

Of course, the real draw for the Museum of Play is the National Toy Hall of Fame. Each year a new batch of toys is inducted into the Hall, with great interest being taken by toy fans all across America. A list of the inductees will make even a grown man's eyes water with the mists of nostalgia!

1998	Barbie, Tinkertoy, Crayola Crayons, Erector Set, Etch A Sketch, Frisbee, Monopoly, Play-Doh, marbles, teddy bear, Lego
1999	Hula Hoop, Radio Flyer Wagon, View-Master, Duncan Yo-Yo, Lincoln Logs
2000	Mr. Potato Head, jump rope, jacks, bicycle, Slinky
2001	Tonka Trucks, Silly Putty
2002	Jigsaw puzzle, Raggedy Ann
2003	Alphabet blocks, checkers
2004	G.I. Joe, rocking horse, Scrabble
2005	Candy Land, Jack in the Box
2006	The cardboard box (!), Lionel Trains, Easy-Bake Oven
2007	Atari, the kite, Raggedy Andy
2008	The stick, baby doll, skateboard
2009	The ball, Big Wheels, Nintendo Game Boy
2010	Playing cards, the Game of Life

REFERENCE FILE

Much can be found regarding Susan B. Anthony's connection with the city of Rochester in the monograph *Failure Is Impossible: The Legacy of Susan B. Anthony* by Ruth Rosenberg-Naparsteck (in the quarterly *Rochester History* 57, no. 4 [Fall 1995], published by the Rochester Public Library). Another book, *The City of Frederick Douglass: Rochester's African-American People and Places* by Eugene E. DuBois (Landmark Society of Western New York, 1995), is an excellent companion piece illuminating the life and local connection of Susan B. Anthony's tea partner.

Pepsy M. Kettavong is one of Rochester's favorite public art contributors. He places his work in a natural setting, which invites interaction with the average passerby. Another of his popular sculptures is Nathaniel Rochester: Founder of the City, located in a small pocket park at the corner of South and Alexander Avenues.

Rochester is filled with great public art, designed and created by some of America's most famous artists and sculptors. For a list, with photos, visit http://www.rochesterpublicart.com.

THE PRESIDENT'S WHISKERS

The Lincoln-Bedell Statue, Westfield

The western rim of New York State skirts some of the most beautiful areas in the mid-Atlantic region. With Great Lakes on the horizon, inland lakes abounding, rolling foothills rippling off into the distance, and miles and miles of grape vineyards everywhere, this is truly a stunning region of the Empire State. Many small to mid-sized towns and villages dot the area, with cloud-piercing church spires, Victorian architecture, and wide, tree-lined Main Streets being the norm. Westfield, New York, is no exception.

With a population of around 5,000 people, Westfield evokes a Thomas Kinkade–type of lifestyle. A fenced-off town square invites neighborly meet-ups, and Mom and Pop shops along the quaint business district evoke a nostalgia of bygone days. Two distinct historic districts mark the importance of the community, albeit a long ago importance. The War of 1812, ancient Native American portages, early businesses, and the nearness (less than a mile) to Lake Erie all played key roles in the development of Westfield, but it was two distinctly different developments that put the town on the map: grape juice and Abraham Lincoln's beard!

In 1869, resident Dr. Thomas Welch perfected the pasteurization of the table grape. The Concord grape had been widely produced in the fertile soil of Western New York for years, but with this new development, grape juice skyrocketed as the drink of choice for Americans of all ages. First showcased in 1893 at the World's Columbian Exposition in Chicago, demand for the new beverage ran unchecked across the nation. Thomas's son Charles built a large grape juice plant in Westfield, and history was made. Today, as it was then, Westfield is recognized as the grape juice capital of the world.

The popularity of grape juice was aided greatly by the temperance move-ment, which was sweeping the nation after the turn of the century. As a substi-tute for wine, grape juice was the officially sanctioned alternate drink at dinner parties and soirees of all class levels. In 1913, US Secretary of State William Jen-nings Bryant chose to serve Welch's juice instead of wine at diplomatic functions in Washington, DC, and the imprimatur of a member of the president's Cabinet certified Welch's Grape Juice as a true business success!

Surrounding Chautauqua County hosts over twenty thousand acres of grape vineyards, more than any other American county outside of California. Several Westfield grape growers have quickly evolved into private-label wine companies that offer winery tours and wine-tasting events.

So much for the grape juice. Now for Abe Lincoln's beard!

THE STATUE

Grace Bedell was eleven years old when, on October 15, 1860, she wrote a letter to then-candidate Abraham Lincoln, urging him to grow his facial whiskers to make him appear more presidential. Here is what the little Westfield girl wrote to the great man from Illinois:

To: Hon. A.B. Lincoln
Dear Sir:
My father has just come home from the fair and brought home your picture and Mr. Hamlin's. I am a little girl only 11 years old, but want you should be President of the United States very much so I hope you won't think me very bold to write to such a great man as you are. Have you any little girls about as large as I am if so give them my love and tell her to write to me if you cannot answer this letter. I have got 4 brothers and part of them will vote for you any way and if you let your whiskers grow I will try and get the rest of them to vote for you would look a great deal better for your face is so thin. All the ladies like whiskers and they would tease their husbands to vote for you and then you would be President. My father is going to vote for you and if I was a man I would vote for you to but I will try to get every one to vote for you that I can. I think that rail fence around your picture makes it look very pretty. I have got a little baby sister she is nine weeks old and is just as cunning as can be. When you direct your letter direct to Grace Bedell, Westfield, Chautauqua County New York.
    I must not write any more. Answer this letter right off. Good-bye
                                        Grace Bedell
                                        Westfield, New York

Both the letter and the little girl's honest observation intrigued Lincoln. He penned the following reply:

Miss Grace Bedell:
My dear little Miss,
Your very agreeable letter of the 15th is received.
    I regret the necessity of saying I have no daughters. I have three sons—one seventeen, one nine, and one seven, years of age. They, with their mother, constitute my whole family.

As to the whiskers, having never worn any, do you not think people
would call it a piece of silly affectation if I were to begin it now?

Your very sincere well-wisher,

A. Lincoln

To the surprise of almost everyone, he showed up in Westfield on February 16, 1861, on his way from Springfield, Illinois, to the White House. As the train stopped at the depot, the tall, fully bearded president-elect appeared from his private car waving his stovepipe hat to the huge crowd there to greet him. He asked for silence and called out for Grace. She was there with her two sisters, Alice and Helen, and the little girl was ushered up to meet Mr. Lincoln. He reached down and kissed her cheek and asked her if she approved of his beard. She said yes, and a huge cheer went up from the assemblage.

The encounter between the president and the little girl is memorialized in Westfield today at the Lincoln-Bedell Statue Park, located in the downtown area at the intersection of NYS Routes 20 and 394. The depiction is humorous and poignant at the same time; the towering, bearded Lincoln holds his trademark hat in one hand and stretches out his other in greeting as he approaches the little girl, dressed in her Sunday finest with a ribboned straw hat atop her curly head and a bouquet of flowers clutched in her hands. A shy smile hints at her unease in the public spotlight. A pretty brick plaza sets the area off from the businesses on this corner, and a plaque describes the real-life event depicted in sculptor Don Sottile's bronze tableau. Sottile, a native of Westfield, dedicated the statue on July 10, 1999.

An interesting side note to this historic event is the fact that Abraham Lincoln made only two train trips between his Illinois home and Washington, DC. One was this trip, encountering little Grace Bedell, on his way *to* the White House in 1861. The other trip was his funeral train procession taking his body home *from* the White House following his assassination.

Grace Bedell eventually married a Union veteran and moved to Delphos, Kansas, where she lived to be eighty-seven years old. For more than seven decades she was constantly asked about her presidential encounter, and she delighted in telling and retelling the story of "the president's whiskers." A monument in the center of Delphos recreates her letters, and a marker at the city's entrance reads: "Delphos: The Home of Lincoln's Little Correspondent."

The original copy of Grace's letter to the president is in the possession of the Burton Historical Collection of the Detroit Public Library. The original Lincoln reply to the little girl is owned by an anonymous private collector. Obviously, both of these documents are worth a fortune.

WHILE HERE

The former headquarters of Welch's Grape Juice can be seen across the street from the Lincoln-Bedell Statue Park. At the time of the publication of this book, the building was unoccupied.

The Westfield area is saturated with wineries, lakefront activities, and historic sights, all spreading along a thirty-mile corridor from Chautauqua Lake north to Lake Erie. Westfield is at the second to final exit of the New York State Thruway.

The famed Chautauqua Institution is just a few short minutes south of Westfield and is definitely worth a visit. A private gated community open to the public nine weeks out of the year (summer), Chautauqua is a wealthy, sophisticated lakeside retreat well over a century old. Built for the purpose of teaching Sunday school teachers, the institution today hosts four hundred permanent residents and thousands of visitors each year. Buildings housing music camps, dance troupes, and theatrical companies pepper the 750-acre campus. A six thousand-seat amphitheater annually welcomes such popular stars as Bill Cosby and Neil Sedaka as well as visiting symphonies and touring plays. The grand Athenaeum Hotel on the grounds is the largest wooden building in the United States east of the Mississippi River. Stunning mansions with landscaped lawns crowd the narrow passageways (vehicles are frowned upon) of the writer-named streets (Emerson Street, Longfellow Lane, etc.). Celebrities, millionaires, and captains of industry have been visiting Chautauqua for decades, and every president for three decades, up to and including Bill Clinton, has made a visit to this truly unique place. More than two hundred thousand people come to Chautauqua each year to enjoy the entertainment, lectures, and symposiums offered here.

Perhaps the oddest feature of Chautauqua is the scale replica of the Holy Land known as Palestine Park. It runs along the shore of Chautauqua Lake and depicts the countries, towns, mountains, and rivers of the regions in the Bible. The lake represents the Mediterranean Sea, a river (Jordan River) runs through the middle of it, and communities such as Bethlehem and Jerusalem are marked by tiny white blocks (for buildings). The park was laid out in 1874 to aid in the instruction of the Bible to Sunday school teachers. It covers nearly four hundred feet and rises and falls on a scale of 1.75 feet to one mile of the original territory. Visitors are invited to hike along the Jordan valley and traverse the Holy Land at this truly unique and one-of-a-kind attraction.

REFERENCE FILE

The story of the little girl and the president is perfect for the writer's imagination. Even more fittingly it is the fodder for several award-winning and popular children's books. Among the best are *Mr. Lincoln's Whiskers* by Karen B. Winnick (Boyds Mills Press, 1999), *Lincoln's Little Girl: A True Story* by Fred Trump (Boyds Mills Press, 2000), and *Grace's Letters to Lincoln* by Peter and Connie Roop (Hyperion Books for Children, 1998).

The community has a very informative Web site with photos at http://www.westfieldny.com. Don Sottile's Web site shows many of his commissions including the Lincoln-Bedell statue. Find it at http://www.sottilesculpture.com.

20

THE WORKINGMAN'S FRIEND

The McKinley Statue, Walden

Walden, New York, evidences the long arm of New York City in a real way. Located an hour north of the city, it teems and bustles in a hurried manner. Cars zip in and out of small storefronts, and people yell at each other from car to car. Suburban housing developments are lined up at the edge of town with same-looking homes on tree-named streets, and a general buzz hovers over the town almost constantly. With only about 6,000 residents, Walden seems larger than it really is. Wallkill State Prison, a large medium-security prison, is located just outside of town and is a major employer. The area has much in the way of natural beauty and is uniquely situated just outside the Catskill Mountain Park, right at its doorstep for easy activity access.

The Walden area (in Orange County) has in the past been the real economic engine that drove the prosperity of the region. Early settlers (including Jacob Walden, who gave the town his name) dammed up the Wallkill River to create a waterpower source for many successful wool mills stretching for miles out of town. Known locally as Walden Mills, the giant power station built to drive this industry is still here, although the mills and the wool are long gone. The making of knives was a profitable niche industry in the 1800s, and several knife factories rehabilitated the empty woolen mills. Soon Walden became one of the premier knife and blade manufacturing centers in the country, and the area became known familiarly as Knife Town. The New York Knife Company, the largest of the knife companies, was the major source of all cutlery bought for Union Army soldiers.

In 1894, the Wilson-Gorman Tariff Act went into effect, substantially lowering the money charged on foreign products entering the United States. This

opened the floodgates for cheap knives and flatware to enter the country (primarily from Germany) and thereby threatened the American industry, in particular the eggs-in-one-basket community known as Knife Town. Robert Bradley, the chairman of the New York Knife Company, went to Washington to personally plead with his old friend, President William McKinley, for some relief from the impending financial disaster facing Walden. The president responded favorably by signing the Dingley Tariff Act on July 24, 1897, which returned the status quo of excise tax rates. In tribute to his old Walden friend, McKinley made this the first piece of major legislation signed during his presidency. The company and the town were saved from obliteration, and the gratitude of the local folks was manifested in a giant tribute to their presidential workingman's friend, William McKinley. Company founder Bradley paid for the statue.

THE STATUE

It is not surprising that there are more statues to President George Washington than there are for any other chief executive. Abraham Lincoln is not far behind. Presidents Theodore Roosevelt, Franklin Roosevelt, John F. Kennedy, and Ronald Reagan have also triggered a statuary bonanza among the sculptors of America.

But why so many for our twenty-fifth president, William McKinley?

Maybe it is because our country was engulfed with the grief brought on by the unsuspected assassination of a popular leader (McKinley was so well liked he was elected twice). Maybe it is because he was loved for helping our nation usher in a dynamic new century (he was shot in 1901). Or maybe it was just because, well, darn it, people liked him! Certainly the artists who benefited from huge commissions to carve out his stern, serious, foreboding likeness liked him *a lot* (as for McKinley's humorless visage, some suggest that he was the model for the fictional Wizard in L. Frank Baum's *Wizard of Oz*, which was written during McKinley's second term in office). A quick search turns up statues or busts of President McKinley in Adams, Massachusetts; Arcata, California; Philadelphia; Antietam, Maryland; Honolulu; Buffalo; and Canton, Dayton, and Columbus, Ohio (McKinley was a native of Ohio and a former governor there). The first statue to the fallen president was erected in Muskegon, Michigan, on May 23, 1902, barely eight months after his death!

This entry in *Monumental New York!* focuses on the most unusual of all the statues of President William McKinley. It is in Walden, the smallest location of a statue to him and maybe the only statue erected in his honor *before* his death. It is a great story!

The severe profile of our twenty-fifth president dominates a tiny, grassy corner in downtown Walden. Sculpted by Henry Kitson (whose most famous work is the Minuteman statue on the green in Lexington, Massachusetts), it stands nearly fifteen feet tall and is a most remarkable likeness of McKinley, right down to the furrowed brow, the stocky build, and the impeccable dress he was known for (you can see the pleats in his finely tailored trousers). The president is clutching a massive standard with the American flag draped over his shoulder. A large eagle tops the flag standard. The granite boulder pedestal reads simply: "McKinley, Erected by the Workingmen of Walden."

The incongruity of the placement of the statue is not slight. It is at a busy intersection of the two main roads going through downtown Walden. The statue faces Orange Street and stands next to one of the oldest buildings in Walden. An architecturally stylish capstone on the bright red building reads "The Fowler Building 1898," although on the day I visited the president it was the home of a garishly lit Chinese restaurant! Across the street is the historic Walden Post Office, with a cornerstone set by Andrew Mellon, the only secretary of the Treasury to serve under three presidents. Behind the president are a series of convenience stores.

Washington's statues may be impressive, and Lincoln's may be inspiring, but this bigger-than-life tribute to William McKinley is certainly offered up with the most gratitude and thanks by the smallest group of Americans: the workingmen of Walden.

WHILE HERE

Using Orange County as your base, I would have to say that three day trips must be included in any visit to Walden or the surrounding area. All are in the county, and as diverse as they are, they are all fun and interesting. The US Military Academy at West Point is twenty-five miles away, and an entire day here would still not let you see everything. The chapel, the sports playing fields, the monuments to military units from different wars, the brass quarters (where the officers live), the cemetery (where the buried include astronauts, soldiers, spies, writers, and more, including General George Armstrong Custer), the unparalleled Hudson River vistas—all make a trip to West Point unforgettable (http://www.usma.edu).

For another fun day trip, go biking. I mean, really biking! Orange County Choppers is the maker of the nation's most eye-popping tricked-out motorcycles. As seen on the hit television show *American Chopper*, these choppers have been commissioned by movie stars, sports legends, millionaires, and others. A special memorial World Trade Center bike features metal from the fallen skyscrapers, and a $150,000 deluxe Air Force bike was recently created as a recruitment tool for the service. The bike is a ten-foot-long model of an Air Force F-22 Raptor fighter jet. The OCC's showroom is located on Route 17K just five miles outside of Walden (http://www.orangecountychoppers.com).

Finally, a day must be spent just twelve miles south of Walden on Route 208 in Washingtonville, home of the Brotherhood Winery, America's Oldest Winery. This quaint, European-style winery is a fun tourist destination, with shopping, dining, historic buildings, wine tasting, and an amazing array of original underground vaults to explore. They are famous for their pinot noir varieties. President Bill Clinton chose the winery's award-winning Riesling to be served at many of his White House state functions (http://www.brotherhoodwinery.net).

REFERENCE FILE

An informative book about the history of Walden and neighboring Maybrook is *Walden and Maybrook: Images of America* by Mark Newman (Arcadia Publishing, 2001). The book includes many archival photos of the area, including the early knife manufacturing plants.

For information about sculptor Henry Kitson visit http://www.askart.com.

21

SUNFLOWERS AND ROSES
SUNY Oneonta 9/11 Memorial, Oneonta

Oneonta, New York, has a *lot* of plusses in its column.

A clean and green industry base, which has rolled back the smokestack grime of three generations of railroaders in the past, draws employees from as far as seventy-five miles away. Now decidedly literate and high-tech, a half-century ago Oneonta was one of the major railroad hubs in the Northeast, hosting a true wonder of the railroad world, the largest locomotive roundhouse ever built. Today, companies such as Corning and Astrocom have replaced the legions of soot-covered Italian train yard laborers with sterile-clothed techies pulling in higher-than-average hourly wages. Oneonta is the home of two colleges more than a hundred years old, Hartwick College and SUNY Oneonta. These institutes of higher learning enroll more than seven thousand students a year, mostly from faraway Downstate. Until recently the city was the home of the Oneonta Tigers, a Class A minor league baseball affiliation that, with a few team name changes, goes back almost to the creation of the league, and all under the same family last name, Nader (also a father and son mayoral combination).

With a sprawling, busting-at-the-seams commercial district on "the other side of the river," downtown Oneonta is also now slowly emerging as a haven for specialty restaurants, pubs, live music, and cafés, after a period of benign neglect. A. O. Fox Memorial Hospital has been a loyal neighbor to Oneontans for more than a hundred years, offering complete, modern, innovative medical care of every possible kind. Oneonta is the media center for its sprawling, rural county (Otsego County) with four radio stations and the largest circulating newspaper in the region, *The Daily Star*.

Oneonta proudly claims the birthing rights to IBM, which had its start here with a new-fangled time clock machine used by Harlow E. Bundy during his tenure as Oneonta's postmaster in 1889. His gadget was later patented, and Bundy Electric Manufacturing Company, the great granddaddy of Big Blue, was formed. Legend has it that the early founders of the company went door to door selling the shares of the start-up company for pennies on the dollar. Now, of course, the homes where the owners "bit" are the sprawling mansions that dot the town's historic Center City area along beautiful Walnut Street, Millionaire's Row.

A brand new, multimillion dollar arts complex in the downtown area, the Foothills Performing Arts Center, adds to the prospects of a bright future for the City of the Hills.

THE MONUMENT

When I began the research for this book, I knew I would find unusual tributes to unknown men and women, memorials to unknown events, and monuments in (hitherto) unknown places. I also knew that I would find a plethora of tributes to the horrible events of September 11, 2001, a date that no person can escape from, emotionally, spiritually, financially, or otherwise. Virtually every major community across America now has a 9/11 memorial to the victims of our nation's saddest day, but none so much so as here in New York State. From Long Island to Ground Zero to the wilds of the Adirondack Mountains, plaques, statues, memorials, and tributes are everywhere.

In Rochester they remember the date with a memorial flag; in tiny Churchville, they have erected a clock tower. In Albany at the New York State Museum, people solemnly pass by a wrecked New York City fire truck, hauled from the smoking ruins of the Twin Towers. Memorial plaques, eagles, honor rolls, and other sentiments fan out across the state, etched with the names of the dead and inscribed with words of inspiration. I knew I had to include one in this book.

I chose the memorial on the campus of SUNY Oneonta to represent all of them. Located on the northern quad of the SUNY campus, across from the Hunt College Union, there stand two giant towers, plain, grim, stark, and somehow, warmly comforting.

Artist and sculptor Charles Bremer of Otego created these twin towers out of twenty-five tons of cast concrete. They rise twelve feet skyward like silent sentinels amid the hurly-burly of campus life and honor seven victims of the disaster with ties to the college community. Atop each tower, at precisely (to scale) the exact location of the planes crashing into them, curiously consoling emblems adorn the towers. On the south tower, near the sixtieth-floor impact zone, Bremer has fashioned a peaceful sunflower to mark the spot where souls were sent skyward, the sunflower being a mostly southern flower. Near the ninety-first-floor impact zone of the north tower, the artist has placed a rose, decidedly a northern flower, emerging from the crash site. The center of the rose dissolves into an abstract teardrop and heart motif. And that is it. No flags, no eagles, no men in uniform, no smoke, no fire. Two great towers sprouting a rose and a sunflower. The monument is poignant and peaceful and will speak to you. It is magnificent in its simplicity. To me, it represents perfectly all of the hundreds of memorials to that dark day.

WHILE HERE

In downtown Oneonta, you will find a curious piece of public art. It is a smaller version of the Statue of Liberty, in the city's Neahwa Park, right outside the Tigers' ballpark. In the early 1950s, a Kansas City millionaire named J. P. Whitaker made these available to all Boy Scout troops in America to celebrate scouting's fortieth anniversary with a campaign entitled Strengthen the Arm of Liberty. All any town had to do was pony up $350 (plus shipping) and the statue would arrive, without a base. The statues are eight feet tall, weigh nearly three hundred pounds each, and were created by the Friedley-Voshardt Company in Chicago. It is estimated that over one thousand communities ordered them.

A Boy Scout troop in Cheyenne, Wyoming, documented the whereabouts of the remaining statues in 2000. Of the many ordered, less than two hundred remain. The four remaining statues in New York State are in the communities of Oneonta, Schenectady, Utica, and Olean (http://www.cheyennetroop101.org/liberty). Others are always being searched for.

Anchoring the center of a Main Street-in-transition sits the Greater Oneonta Historical Society at the corner of Main and Dietz Streets (the History Center, as it is called). This is a repository of more than five thousand items associated with Old Oneonta and the Susquehanna River region. They have a series of ambitious projects underway, both capital and acquistional. Stroll inside and pick up some local literature and take a look at one of the last existing pianos made in Oneonta; the town was a cigar manufacturing center, too. Look over the architect's handiwork of returning this current building facade back to the nostalgic look of one of its original owners from decades ago, the fondly remembered early twentieth-century Laskaris Candy Shoppe. The History Center is a charming addition to historic downtown (http://www.oneontahistory.org).

Comfy independent bookstores (the Green Toad), aromatic coffee shops (the Latte Lounge), many old-fashioned pie-tossing Italian pizza parlors (Ruffino's, Sal's, Mama Nina's), and inviting niche pubs and restaurants (the Autumn Café, among others) all make this a happening place both at lunch and at night.

While in the park viewing the Statue of Liberty replica, just a few hundred feet away you will find a remarkable piece of history. This little train caboose, encased in glass, is an icon of the transportation industry. Here in Oneonta, in this Little Red Caboose, eight Delaware and Hudson railroad brakemen met to create an organization with the goals of bettering the life of trainmen everywhere. They forged safety and salary demands and created a manifesto of better working conditions for all. From this tiny caboose, in 1883, one of the first railroad unions in the United States, the Brotherhood of Railroad Brakemen, came to be.

REFERENCE FILE

An interesting book about the city is *Oneonta: Then and Now* by Mark Simonson (Arcadia Publishing, 2006). Simonson, also the city's historian, dramatically shows the changes in the city through a comparison of "now and then" photographs and postcards, accompanied by historical text. At the History Center you can also purchase *The Oneonta Roundhouse* by the local author and railroad historian Jim Louden (Square Circle Press, 2011).

Oneonta is located on the southern border of Otsego County along Interstate 88. For information, photos, and maps of the college campus at SUNY Oneonta (which hosts the 9/11 memorial), visit http://www.oneonta.edu.

22

THE GOLDEN PLATES

Hill Cumorah Moroni Monument, Palmyra

As the Erie Canal crept east and west across Upstate New York, small trading posts turned into villages, and villages blossomed into small cities. Although the canal is no longer a commercial waterway, it is easy to see how little map dot communities owed their existence to the canal (much like the life and death decisions concerning interstate highway exit locations today: if you get one, you thrive; if not, you are forgotten). Names like Camillus, Lockport, Rome, Pittsford, Macedon, Clyde, Elbridge, and others all popped up along the "ditch" and became vital, thriving centers of commerce for the duration of the canal's operation, from the early 1800s to the early 1900s, when the railroads and highways usurped the canals' duties as an overland hauler route.

Palmyra, New York, a pleasant village of about 7,000 residents, is a gorgeous reminder of the days of "old canal times." Mills, depots, warehouses, and small shops line the main business district of Palmyra, echoing the days when the streets were crowded with immigrants passing through and commercial buyers and sellers hawking their wares. Today, the village boasts old stone buildings, wide tree-shaded avenues, and flower-box laden storefronts. The largest coverlet collection in America is housed in an old newspaper building on William Street. So vast is this collection that it takes more than six years to completely revolve the colorful and exquisitely stitched covers for public display. At 140 Market Street is the amazing 1816 Phelps General Store, one of the finest original examples of a nostalgic small town store anywhere in America. Historic restoration along the Erie Canal at the port at Palmyra is remarkable and genuinely reflects the community's nickname, the Queen of the Canal. Hundreds pour into Palmyra every

129

fall for a celebration of the canal with its Canal Town Days Festival (http://www
.palmyracanaltowndays.org).

Despite the beauty of this quaint slice of canal history, Palmyra, just a half
hour's drive east of Rochester, will be forever known for a set of golden plates
found just outside of town under the wet grass of a farmer's grazing hill. These
tablets are the impetus for more than a quarter of a million visitors to find their
way to this two-lane village every year.

This is where the Mormons began!

THE MONUMENT

Palmyra is the birthplace of the Church of Jesus Christ of Latter-Day Saints (the
Mormons). Here, in what was then a small, rural trading center, Joseph Smith was
visited by the ancient prophet Moroni and told that the golden plates, on which
Moroni had recorded the history of his people centuries before, were buried in a

hillside just outside of town. He directed Smith to go and dig them up, translate them, and spread the word of the "new" gospel. Smith did this and published the tablets (or golden plates) as the *Book of Mormon: Another Testament of Jesus Christ*.

Everything you ever wanted to know about Moroni, Joseph Smith, the golden plates, the printing of the book, and the dissemination of the word can be found right here, just two miles north of the New York State Thruway (exit 43) at Hill Cumorah, the hill where the tablets were buried and "found," and Palmyra itself, a mile north of the hill.

A stunning, state-of-the-art visitors center (constructed in 2002) welcomes thousands of visitors each year to "learn the word" and believe in the miracle. Members of the Latter-Day Saints religion (referred to as "brothers" and "sisters" on their docent badges) effusively welcome you to the center and usher you into an amphitheater where beautiful wall murals depict religious scenes and comfortable seats invite you to sit and spend contemplative moments. A movie plays continuously, telling the story of Joseph Smith's life, his visit by Moroni, the finding of the plates, the persecution he suffered, and the ultimate founding of the Mormon religion (currently the fourth largest organized religion in America with around seven million believers). The atmosphere of the visitors center is Disney-like, and I mean that in a positive way. The attendants, lecturers, and guides are well scrubbed and well dressed, the presentations are colorful and sophisticated, and the facility and grounds are immaculate and litter free. Convenient parking for hundreds of guests is located right at the front door, with a special area for the many tour buses that come to Hill Cumorah by the dozens every weekend.

The Mormons are big business in Palmyra.

High atop the hill behind the visitors center is an awesome, towering golden statue of the Angel Moroni. An arduous climb of about twenty minutes will take you to the peak where the forty-foot-tall statue lords over a breathtaking twenty-five-mile view of the surrounding scenery. The statue was placed here in 1935. Lush plantings and trees planted in the 1930s create an atmosphere of solemnity, disturbed only by the steady stream of visitors from all over the world. The statue is placed at the spot where Joseph Smith supposedly dug up the golden plates in 1823. For the less hardy or handicapped visitor, a winding road travels up the back of the hill to the top for an easy drive to the Moroni statue.

The whole experience, for the Mormon and the simply curious alike, is unusual, unforgettable, and, frankly, a bit odd. To find this theme park-like religious site in such a rural and unheralded area—there is literally nothing around Hill Cumorah for a mile in every direction—is quite eye opening! And this is on a quiet, ordinary weekday. Imagine what it is like here during the festive Hill Cumorah Pageant (http://www.hillcumorah.org), an annual theatrical presentation of the events of Joseph Smith's life, Bible stories, and other religious reenactments. More than ten thousand visitors a day attend the seven performances, which includes hundreds of costumed performers, herds of live animals, Las Vegas–style sets and lighting, rock concert–like sound towers, Hollywood special effects, flying angels, fireworks, an enormous nine-level stage that climbs the hill, and the piped-in music of the famed Mormon Tabernacle Choir! The pageant has been performed to sellout crowds every year, except for when it was suspended during the World War II years, since 1937.

WHILE HERE

The village of Palmyra is home to a wide assortment of Mormon-based venues, all worth a short visit. The Sacred Grove, a lush glen of tall trees where it is said Joseph Smith first had a vision of Jesus, is the destination of Mormon pilgrims by the thousands each year. At 217 Main Street in the village is the printing press site where the plates were transcribed and printed up. The Palmyra Temple, the Joseph Smith Farm, and more are highlighted throughout the town with directional signs and New York State historical markers. Some Smith graves are also in Palmyra on Church Street. Not Joseph's though. He is buried at his home site in Nauvoo, Illinois. He had been arrested there on charges of suppression of the press for violence against those who disagreed with his religious proclamations. He was jailed in Carthage, Illinois, with his brother, Hyrum. An angry mob of three hundred citizens broke down the doors of the jail and murdered the two on June 27, 1844.

REFERENCE FILE

An interesting book about the history of the Hill Cumorah extravaganza is *This You Must Know! America's Witness for Christ: The Hill Cumorah Pageant* by Jack Sederholm (Mormon Church, 1979).

The sculptor of the Angel Moroni statue at Hill Cumorah in Palmyra is Torleif S. Knaphus. He was born in Norway and became a follower of the Church of

Latter-Day Saints as a young man (he was baptized in an ice-covered fjord near his home). He later moved to the United States to be near other followers. He was a natural artist and became the religion's unofficial sculptor. He did several works for the Mormons before he created Moroni for their newly purchased site in Upstate New York in the 1920s. A fascinating story is one in which he said an angel of God came down and pointed to one of several drawings of Moroni that Knaphus was trying to decide on. According to the sculptor the angel appeared and gestured to one and said, "This is the one!" These and other stories about Knaphus and the great Moroni sculpture can be found online at http://www.byu.edu.

"I WANT NOTHING!"

The Proctor Eagle Monument, Utica

The hallmark of so many of Upstate New York's mid-sized cities is the decline of their manufacturing and population bases.

Utica is no different.

Early on, Utica was known as the Canal City because of the confluence of so many waterways tracing through the Mohawk Valley and through the city itself, including the Erie Canal, connecting Albany and Buffalo, and the Chenango Canal, cutting through the midsection of the state to connect Utica with Binghamton. Next came the Textile City in the late 1800s when Utica was the center of the growing textile manufacturing industry nationwide. The next century brought General Electric to town and the new Chamber of Commerce moniker the Radio City, heralding the eight thousand GE workers churning out more radios than any other city in the East. This was followed briefly by the St. Louis of the North, when Utica flexed its beer muscles. Several legendary beers called Utica home, many coming from the F. X. Matt Brewing Company, including local favorite Utica Club, which was the first beer sold in America after Prohibition. Then, with the drain of virtually its entire manufacturing base, Utica turned to less tangible slogans and more aesthetic phrases such as the City of the Valley, and the Handshake City.

Ultimately, near its nadir in the latter part of the twentieth century, when its population began a nosebleed descent from around 100,000 residents to the current 60,000, people whispered that Utica was the City That God Forgot.

But this tough, gritty, big-shouldered city is not down and out. Like its sister cities across the region, Utica has plenty of life left in it and is not without hope,

pockets of urban revitalization, a feeling of rebirth, a sense of community, a glorious and fascinating history, and some terrific natural beauty!

Utica is poised for a new beginning. The urban flight of the past decades seems to have been reversed, for various reasons. Falling back on its luminous history as a city of enlightenment and culture, several top-notch art galleries and museums flourish under energetic leadership. A new wave of late-twentieth-century immigrants from Bosnia has added to the distinct international spice of life in the city. In fact, the US State Department lists Utica as the city with the nation's fourth largest concentration (proportionately) of refugees, recognizing that the city's population is now nearly 10 percent war refugees from Bosnia, in addition to the number of Vietnamese, Ukrainian, and Russian immigrants who came to the city in the 1970s.

Tourism is on the rise in both Utica and Oneida County. Within a short drive of the city center, you will find historic race tracks, one of the most successful gambling casinos in the Northeast (Turning Stone Casino), live theater, canal museums, halls of fame, historic landmarks (including the incredible Revolutionary War site at Fort Stanwix in neighboring Rome), hiking trails, some of the best lake and river fishing in America, and even a diamond mine to explore!

Utica is annually in the national sports spotlight when it holds the running of the Boilermaker, America's biggest, best, and most awarded 15K road race. Tens of thousands of runners converge on Utica's streets for the running of this race, which began in 1976. The race ends at the F. X. Matt Brewery, where an after-race celebration of legendary proportions ensues. *Runner's World Magazine* called Utica's Boilermaker one of the top, if not the top, 15K road races in America. An offshoot to the race was the establishment of the National Distance Running Hall of Fame at 114 Genesee Street. The first class of inductees in 1998 included Olympians Frank Shorter and Joan Benoit as well as Bill Rodgers, a legendary marathoner perhaps most associated with the Boston Marathon.

THE MONUMENT

Few cities in America have benefited as much from the financial largesse of a single family as Utica has from the Proctor family. Some communities come close. Cooperstown is basically the fiefdom of the fabulously wealthy Clark family of

Singer sewing machine fortune, and to great and benevolent results. The Roosevelts of Hyde Park, the Russell Sages (mostly Mrs.) of Troy, the Morton banking family of Rhinebeck, and the Eastman clan and their film fortune in Rochester have left their family seals, in one way or another, all over their hometowns.

But the Proctors . . . now they are big!

Wealthy Thomas Redfield Proctor landed in Utica shortly after serving in the Civil War, and he arrived with a shopping list in his well-lined pockets. Hotels, mansions, businesses, and dairy farms were snatched up and put in the family ledger. The Bagg's Hotel and Butterfield House were two of Utica's showplace hotels, and Proctor added more to the gilt of these historic properties after purchasing them. He married the well-heeled Maria Munson Williams in 1891. He founded a couple of banks in Utica. They had no surviving children.

Younger half-brother Frederick Towne Proctor followed Thomas to Utica a few short years later and entered the furniture making business. He also married well and married close. In 1894 he married his sister-in-law, Rachel Williams, Maria's older sister.

The Williams sisters were the daughters of Helen Munson Williams (1824–1894), a wealthy and generous socialite and philanthropist, whose passion was fine arts and jewelry. Helen Williams was a major force in Utica and sat on virtually every major institutional and philanthropic board in the city. Her two daughters and their husbands (they were half-brothers, remember) combined to make up one of the most powerful, influential, and benevolent family networks in Upstate New York, and the results of their efforts continue to cast a glittering shine over their beloved city.

Both couples saw their fortunes rise as Utica grew into a major city in the Upstate New York region, situated hard along the Erie Canal, the major business route between Albany and Buffalo. The couples bought side-by-side mansions. Frederick and Rachel, like their familial neighbors, also were childless.

The Proctor brothers and the Williams sisters made for one of the most formidable philanthropic forces that Upstate New York has ever seen.

You can't say Utica without saying Munson Williams Proctor!

High atop Roscoe Conkling Park (Conkling was a Utica congressman, senator, and mayor), near the southern edge of the city, one gets an extraordinary view of the city and the Mohawk Valley beyond. The vista, on a clear day, extends almost fifty miles. It is stunning.

Here, situated on a sliver of land between two of Utica's oldest cemeteries, is a towering and regal tribute to Thomas Proctor, the Proctor Eagle.

Standing alone, wings outstretched, talons bared, this bald eagle surveys the surroundings with fierce pride and nobility. The bronze eagle is perched atop a fifteen-foot-tall marble column, with historic descriptive plaques on either side. These plaques speak of an actual, incredible event in Proctor's life. The plaque reads:

> This monument is erected to the memory and honor of Thomas Redfield Proctor by his wife. He was an incorruptible citizen and a pure patriot. If asked what he wished in reward for any good public deed, he answered, "I want nothing!" An American eagle in a cage was once offered to him. He bought it and liberated it on the 4th of July. It paused a moment and then took its flight. He [Proctor] was also given his liberty on the 4th of July 1920 and went the way the bird did, seeking his native element and the true Father of his country.

The sculptor is Charles Keck, and it is a remarkable tribute both in style and place.

To reach the Proctor Eagle, travel south along Utica's grand thoroughfare, Genesee Street, to the edge of the city limits. Along the way you will pass the hulking State Office Building, the nostalgic 1928 Stanley Theater, and the Utica Public Library. Once you pass the statue to General Pulaski, you will veer left onto Oneida Street and continue for a mile and a half. You will then see two cemeteries next to each other. First is New Forest Cemetery, and next to it is the old Forest Hill Cemetery. If you look carefully, you will see sandwiched in between the two entrances to these cemeteries a large set of wrought iron gates with the letters "R" and "C" on them. This is the very narrow entrance to Roscoe Conkling Park. Drive through the gates and go to the very top of the mountain to find the well-marked Proctor Eagle.

From this alpine aerie overlooking Utica, turn around and peer into Forest Hill Cemetery, just over a chain link fence. The massive mausoleum facing you belongs to James Schoolcraft Sherman, Utica native and President William Howard Taft's vice president.

Next to Sherman's grave is the elaborate plot holding the ornate graves of those so very well-known Uticans: Munson, Williams, and Proctor.

WHILE HERE

Utica has more public statuary than any other city of its size in Upstate New York. The tributes are everywhere and are very interesting. Throughout the downtown area are towering statues to everyone from Copernicus to Columbus to Pulaski. But Memorial Parkway, which crosses Oneida Street on your way to Roscoe Conkling Park, is really wonderful. The mile-long median features many memorials and historic monuments all along the walking path.

Along the parkway you will see the Swan Fountain, sculpted by Frederick MacMonnies, a prolific artist and student of Augustus Saint-Gaudens; several beautiful war memorials; and busts and statues of famous Americans. One gripping memorial pays tribute to America's missing prisoners of war. The depiction, of a soldier being abused by the enemy, is particularly moving. The gold-lettered legend on the monument reads: "We Speak for Those Who Can't."

The Munson Williams Proctor Art Institute is a regional treasure. Established in 1919 by the Proctors and the Williams families, this multibuilding facility is one of Upstate New York's most pleasant diversions. Encompassing the original Proctor mansion and then added onto with a building designed by famed architect Philip Johnson, this gallery is full of priceless decorative arts and paintings.

The early family members scoured the world collecting watches made of precious jewels and created by the world's most famous jewelers. The array is dazzling. It is considered to be perhaps the greatest intact timepiece collection in the world.

Along with Thomas and Frederick's three hundred timepieces, original paintings from great masters adorn the walls of this big-city museum tucked away in rural Upstate New York. Artists represented include Jackson Pollock, Mark Rothko, Winslow Homer, Andy Warhol, Edward Hopper, Frederic Church, and Georgia O'Keefe. Hudson River master Thomas Cole's four-painting allegorical masterpiece *The Voyage of Life* is also at the museum (http://www.mwpai.org).

REFERENCE FILE

For a gorgeous look at the presentations made to the Munson Williams Proctor Art Institute, see *Jewels of Time: Watches from the Munson-Williams-Proctor Art Institute* (Munson Williams Proctor Institute, 2001).

Charles Keck was a prolific sculptor whose works are in public parks, museums, statehouses, and private collections. Perhaps his most famous commission, seen by millions over the years, is his stirring statue of the chaplain of the famed Fighting Sixty-Ninth Infantry, Father Patrick Duffy, located in Times Square. For information on this most public of public works visit http://www.nycgovparks.org.

24

"UNDERSTANDING IS JOYOUS"
The Sagan Planet Walk Memorial, Ithaca

THE PLACE

Ithaca, New York, is the largest city in Upstate New York that is not located along a major interstate highway. It can be quite tricky navigating the winding roads and hills on your trek to this community of about 30,000 residents, but when you arrive it is certainly well worth the journey.

Unlike any other city in the state, Ithaca weds the sophisticates with the rubes, the naturalists with the CEOs, the free thinkers with the rigid textbookers, and, in general, the urbanites with the suburbanites. The city is a minor "Switzerland" in that it is cut off from the rest of the state geographically, with no major highways, rail links, or riverways servicing it over the years. But what has grown in this insular haven is a city of intelligence, refinement, cleverness, and natural beauty.

The city is at the foot of beautiful Cayuga Lake, one of the largest of the famed Finger Lakes (some say the "foot" while others argue it is at the "head" of the lake; for the record it lies at the southern end of the lake). Steep hills and waterfront flats compete for the spectacular landscape vistas within the city limits. Cornell University, one of the greatest colleges in the world, is located on the steep escarpments overlooking the lake and the downtown area. Views from any corner of the 750-acre campus are beautiful.

Cornell University, with its twenty-five thousand students and faculty, is really a city within a city. Separated from the rest of Ithaca by steep uphill roads and gorges, the campus is studded with stunning Gothic and Neoclassical buildings designed by noted architects. Landscaping is gorgeous, and pathways crisscross the quads, giving the whole campus a small-town feeling.

It was founded by Ezra Cornell in 1865, and since then has educated and sent out into the world hundreds of elected officials, groundbreaking scientists, renowned educators, and world leaders. Among the college's alumni are forty living Nobel laureates! Famous graduates (known as "Cornellians") are the Supreme Court Justice Ruth Bader Ginsburg, Henry Heimlich (of the lifesaving maneuver), the pediatrician Benjamin Spock, the inventor of the iPod Jonathan Rubinstein, the writer Kurt Vonnegut, the first female US Attorney General Janet Reno, and the actors Christopher Reeve (*Superman*) and Frank Morgan (*The Wizard of Oz*).

An area called Collegetown provides for all of the needs of this inner city, from restaurants to medical facilities. Neighboring Ithaca College, founded in 1892, is another stellar seat of learning, and the combination of Ithaca College and Cornell University gives the city proper a certain joie de vivre, a certain buzz throughout the community that is infectious.

In the busy downtown area, Ithaca Commons is the center of social and business get-togethers. A roughly four-block area of clothing stores, bookstores, ethnic restaurants, coffee shops, and trendy (yet not mass marketed) specialty shops all make for a delightful pedestrian green space in the heart of the busy city.

Outdoor activities are mainly of the "clean" type. Among the favorite pastimes are sailing on the beautiful waters of Cayuga Lake, biking and hiking the trails of the surrounding mountains, and going deep down in any of the numerous ice-age gorges (as the ubiquitous bumper sticker says, "Ithaca Is Gorges!").

Ithaca has a lively entertainment scene, as one would expect with thousands of students in-house. Artists of world repute are an everyday happenstance in the city, and a Pulitzer Prize–winning author, a Grammy Award–winning singer, or a Tony Award–winning play is usually featured in the city's list of coming events.

The recently reopened State Theater, in the Commons, recalls the golden age of vaudeville in the 1920s and 1930s. Currently being restored by the city, the State is a wondrous example of the style of the glory days of live theater. The interior ceiling is painted with an exotic Moorish design, hundreds of tiny lights throughout the interior of the roof evoke a starry desert evening, and one of the first commercial "cloud machines" made a night at the State a dreamy experience. Also proudly featured is one of the largest theater organs in the country, built for $26,000 by the Link Organ Company of Binghamton. If the doors are shut at the State, peer inside the old stained-glass front windows and see the restoration in progress and marvel at the cute little round box office replete with Art Deco flourishes. The large neon marquee, though in poor condition, can still stir the soul of any lover of old-time show business.

It is not unusual to happen upon a piece of public art in downtown Ithaca. Modern, formless statues, ethereal fountains, and "tree art" surrounded by poetry readers, skateboarders, and strolling musicians add up to give this city a lively and interesting heartbeat.

Right in the geographical center of business district, where all sidewalks and paths intersect, is the most uncommon Commons site.

It is our galaxy!

THE MEMORIAL

Carl Sagan's show *Cosmos* was PBS's most-watched television show of all time. Period. Take that, Sesame Street!

Sagan, a beloved host and writer for the PBS show *Cosmos*, was space's greatest cheerleader. Possessed of a boyish charm, an ebullient personality, and the naturalness of your favorite science teacher, Sagan brought the mysteries and wonders of space into the living rooms of more than six hundred million viewers world wide, since the astronomer and scientist first began hosting *Cosmos* in 1980. Carl Sagan was space's first rock star! The show won an Emmy and a Peabody award.

Sagan did much in his short life and career (he died of pneumonia on December 20, 1996, at the age of sixty-two). He was a prolific writer, an important advisor to NASA, a champion of human rights (he was arrested numerous times protesting against the Vietnam War and against nuclear proliferation), and (here comes the Ithaca connection) a popular and beloved resident and teacher in Ithaca.

Carl Sagan began his association with the city as a teacher at Cornell in 1968, becoming a full professor there in 1971. During these turbulent times on all campuses in the United States, Sagan's presence at Cornell was a perfect fit. His classes (astronomy, space sciences, planetary studies) were a distraction from the fractious public debate going on in the streets about war and social evils (all of which he was deeply concerned with), and his classes quickly became the most popular on campus (though many hundreds applied, just a handful were chosen). His campus activities were high profile, and his persona, with hair a little bit over the collar in the back, the buoyancy of youth forever with him, and a naturalness that made him comfortably accessible to student and teacher alike, made him one of the giants of his tenure at Cornell.

The Carl Sagan Memorial Planetary Walk is one of the oddest, and yet most fitting, tributes to a person I found in my travels for *Monumental New York!* It is an exact replica of our solar system spread out over three-quarters of a mile, emanating from the center of the popular Ithaca Commons shopping and entertainment area. Because of the small size of the area, the scale of the galaxy is one mile to *five billion* miles. You can walk from the Sun to the Moon to all the planets and even stand on the spot where Mother Earth is located all within a couple of blocks. As with everything associated with Carl Sagan, it is informative, exciting, and not without a sense of fun.

The informative quotient is filled by maps, pictures, photos, displays, and quotations located on the various, four-foot-tall "monuments" that mark each planet. A round Plexiglas center "hole" represents the galaxy, and you can see in each hole a place marking the respective planet you are at. Diagrams along the sidewalks show you the way on your planetary walk, and people of all ages (especially kids) seem to thrill in skipping and jumping their way from Earth to, say, Mars in just a short distance.

People find this tribute exciting because it is just so darn out of the ordinary! Imagine you are an unsuspecting shopper or diner walking along the Commons on your way back from a show on your way to a restaurant, and you are confronted by something that looks like a cement buoy perched right in the middle of all the shops. You get closer and inspect it and before you know it, you are off on an exciting wander around the solar system. Their incongruous placement startles when one comes upon the complex Planetary Walk here in downtown Ithaca.

And fun . . . well, at any number of places throughout Ithaca, you can purchase ($4) a Planetary Passport with descriptions and commentary by Ann Druyan (Sagan's widow) inside. You can follow along on your route with this booklet, get your passport stamped at each planet, and then redeem your completed passport for a free admission into the Ithaca Sciencenter, one of the most sophisticated, creative, and, yes, fun places for kids of any age in all of Upstate New York!

At the beginning of the Planet Walk, there is a plaque affixed to the first monument, the Sun, which reads: "This scale model of the solar system celebrates the life of Carl Sagan. Astronomer. Teacher. Author. Activist. Who awakened multitudes to the preciousness and fragility of our small planet and the wonders of life in the cosmos as revealed by science."

The plaque is signed: "With love from Ann Druyan, Dorion, Jeremy, Nicholas, Sasha, Sam and Tonio Sagan."

It is a most fitting memorial to a beloved man who truly belonged to the ages.

WHILE HERE

For the weekend visitor to Ithaca, a must-see would be the incredibly beautiful campus of Cornell University, where Carl Sagan taught for many years. The buildings are grand, on a European scale; the scenery and views high above Cayuga's waters are unforgettable; and the sense of history overwhelms you. An interesting stop on your campus tour would be the famous Sage Chapel.

When Ezra Cornell founded his university he directed that it be a nonsectarian place of learning. The Sage Chapel is a cathedral-like structure (yes, it is cross shaped!) that seats eight hundred people and hosts a multitude of speakers on a weekly basis (rather than a single prelate). All of the denominations of the college's students can find solace and spirituality within the walls of this inspirational place. A magnificent, rare Aeolian-Skinner grand organ features four thousand pipes. There are historic plaques throughout paying tribute to great moments and personalities in Cornell's history. Martin Luther King Sr. spoke here in the 1960s. "Daddy King" gave a fiery oration on the civil rights movement to an overflowing crowd of students. Priceless stained glass windows catch the arcing rays of the sun and throw crystals of dancing rainbows into the well of the church. One stained glass window solemnly pays tribute to Andrew Goodman, James Chaney, and Michael Schwerner, the three murdered Mississippi civil rights activists. The window was donated to the college by the Cornell Class of 1961, in honor of their classmate, Mickey Schwerner (Andrew Goodman's parents were also Cornellians).

Up in the choir loft, a small bronze plaque reads: "Life in the barn was very good, night and day, winter and summer, spring and fall, bright days and dull days . . ." A small paragraph from *Charlotte's Web*, follows in this quaint tribute to E. B. White, Cornell Class of 1921 and a member of the Sage Chapel Choir while here.

At the entrance to this august structure, a mausoleum (open to public viewing) holds the remains of Mr. and Mrs. Ezra Cornell. The sarcophagi are so real they make you want to reach out and comb old Ezra's beard and smooth out the marble pillow his head is laying on!

Carl Sagan is buried in Lakeview Cemetery on 605 Eastshore Drive. The cemetery is located just four blocks from Cornell University.

REFERENCE FILE

Sagan's classic *Cosmos* (Ballantine Books) is still a significant seller both in book-stores and online. It was originally published in October 1985.

The most extensive Web site dealing with Carl Sagan's life and works can be found at http://www.carlsagan.com.

25

AMERICA'S CHAMPION

The Seabiscuit Statue, Saratoga Springs

THE PLACE

Why the slogan of the city of Saratoga Springs, New York, is not "We Have It All!" is anybody's guess.

You talk about a cornucopia of wonderful Chamber of Commerce–friendly venues and events! A gorgeous community (more than nine hundred buildings are listed as National Historic Landmarks), every corner of Saratoga offers a treat for the mind and for the eyes. The world-famous Saratoga Race Track, the oldest organized sporting venue in America, opened on August 3, 1863. Yaddo, a four-hundred-acre artists' colony begun in 1900, has hosted more than six hundred artists over the years, including Truman Capote, Sylvia Plath, Aaron Copland, Leonard Bernstein, John Cheever, and many more, including sixty Pulitzer Prize winners. The Saratoga Performing Arts Center, known as SPAC, is a popular rock and pop venue as well as the summer home of the Philadelphia Orchestra and the New York City Ballet. The city is home to the National Museum of Racing and Hall of Fame. The Saratoga Battlefield (just twenty minutes from downtown Saratoga) was the scene of one of the most important military encounters in American history and has been called one of the fifteen most important military battles in world history. Skidmore College is a top liberal arts university with an enrollment of more than 2,500 students. The historic Caffè Lena, the oldest continuously operating coffeehouse in America, has one of the first stages ever graced by a young Bob Dylan. Saratoga really does have it all!

Saratoga Springs (population 30,000) is located just twenty-five miles north of New York's capital, Albany. It got its start because of (as the name says) its springs. Unique healing powers were attributed to the many natural hot springs

that sprouted up all over the city. Because of the quality and numbers of these mineral pools, the city was dubbed the Queen of the Spas by the moneymen of the late nineteenth century who turned this rural village into one of the great playgrounds for the rich and famous. From the As to the Vs (Astors to Vanderbilts), the spas lured the colossuses of wealth and the captains of industry to tiny Saratoga, and with them came the mansions, the fancy restaurants, the massive hotels and resorts, and last but not least, the horse races!

THE STATUE

Saratoga's Union Avenue is one of the most beautiful residential streets in Upstate New York. The length of the avenue is lined, on both sides, with breathtaking mansions sporting wide porches, Victorian architectural details, and meticulously manicured lawns. These are the homes of the "old money" in the city, and because of the proximity to the Saratoga Race Track, many of the great horsemen and women of the time resided here. A leisurely walk from one end of the avenue to the other (ending at Congress Park, the city's magnificent public park, which contains the old casino and several of the famous mineral springs) will afford the visitor a rare and historic look at one of the most incredibly pristine slices of nineteenth-century America. The main entrance to Saratoga Race Track is also on Union Avenue.

The National Museum of Racing and Hall of Fame (191 Union Avenue) was founded in 1950 to honor the great horses, jockeys, trainers, stables, and owners of the sport. The first president was millionaire Cornelius Vanderbilt Whitney; he served from 1950 to 1953. His widow, Marylou Whitney, still presides over much of the social scene during the racing season in Saratoga (the month of August). The Museum and Hall of Fame have grown and expanded over the years to become a state-of-the-art repository of racing memorabilia and nostalgia, all located amid the striped awnings and turreted roofs of this quaint bygone neighborhood.

As with all halls of fame, the wall of honorees, the lists of heroes, and the induction plaques all evoke a different response from each fan that visits. And the lists here are remarkably familiar. For the jockeys there are Eddie Arcaro and Willie Shoemaker, both inducted in 1958. Under the heading of trainers, the name "Burch" certainly sticks out. Grandfather William P. Burch was inducted into the Hall of Fame in the initial class of 1955; followed by his son, Preston (1963) and his grandson, J. Elliot (1980).

As for the horses, the names of the mighty champions come alive, bringing back some of the most exciting moments in any sport: Exterminator, the sorrowful looking horse from Binghamton who went off at 30 to 1 odds to win the 1918 Kentucky Derby, inducted in 1957; Seattle Slew, the only horse to win the Triple Crown while undefeated, inducted in 1981; Gallorette, a Maryland speed demon who was voted the "greatest filly in American racing history" by the American Trainers Association, inducted in 1962; Kelso, the most awarded horse in racing history, inducted in 1967; Regret, one of three members of the same horse family in the Hall; he was inducted in 1957, his father Broomstick in 1956, and his grandfather Ben Brush in 1955; as well as the many legendary headline horses, Man o' War in 1957; Spectacular Bid, 1982; Affirmed, 1980; Whirlaway, 1959; and Secretariat, 1974. But it is the horse whose name follows the year 1958 that is the real superstar at 191 Union Avenue.

Initially trained by the legendary Sunny Jim Fitzsimmons, Seabiscuit was an unlikely hero. Ungainly to look at, lazy at the track, and overshadowed by the great racing steeds of his era (1930s), he underperformed repeatedly until Fitzsimmons threw in the towel and sold him to automobile dealer Charles Howard for $8,000. Under Howard's persistence, with the sage eye of "old hand" trainer Tom Smith and down-on-his-luck Canadian jockey "Red" Pollard in the saddle, this unlikely foursome traveled the byways of America during the Great Depression looking for races, gathering up purses, and catching the eye of a despairing nation in need of a glimmer of hope. The horse had pluck, and their story, like their earnings, began to grow and creep onto the front page of newspapers from New York to Santa Anita and resonate with the average man and woman struggling to make ends meet.

America, it seemed, had a hero on its hands!

On February 19, 1938, Pollard suffered a severe injury to his leg and had to withdraw from his position as Seabiscuit's jockey (he would return after two years of rehabilitation). Friend and fellow jockey George Woolf took over the reins of the increasingly successful racehorse. On November 1, 1938, "the match of the century" took place at Pimlico Race Track (Baltimore) when Seabiscuit finally paired off with the greatest horse of his day, War Admiral (who was Seabiscuit's uncle!). With tens of millions tuning into the live broadcast of the race on the radio, and with a standing-room-only crowd of 42,000 fans packing the race track, Seabiscuit won the day and the hearts of racing fans everywhere with a thrilling four length victory.

More wins would follow, along with riches and fame. Seabiscuit was named Horse of the Year at the end of 1938. A rewarding retirement was waiting for the champion at Ridgewood Ranch in California in 1940. A prolific stud horse, he sired 108 foals. Thousands of fans (including many children) made the pilgrimage to Mendocino County to visit America's Champion, and it was there that he died, on May 17, 1947, just a week shy of his fourteenth birthday.

Several books and movies have documented the inspiring story of Seabiscuit over the years, including a 1949 film starring Shirley Temple. But it was Laura Hillenbrand's 2001 book *Seabiscuit: An American Legend* that really brought the superstar horse back to the forefront for newer generations of Americans. The book was a huge bestseller, and a movie retelling of it, starring Jeff Bridges as Charles Howard, Chris Cooper as trainer Tom Smith, and Tobey Maguire as jockey Red Pollard, garnered several Academy Award nominations, including that for Best Picture. A five-year-old chestnut gelding named Popcorn Deelites performed the dramatic racing scenes as Seabiscuit. (The film lost the coveted Best Picture award to *Lord of the Rings: The Return of the King.*)

A life-sized statue of the champion horse, sculpted by Hughlette "Tex" Wheeler in 1941, stands on the grounds of the National Racing Museum and Hall of Fame. It is completely accessible to the visitor or passerby alike. The giant horse stands in a small plaza surrounded by seasonal plantings. It is lit at night. A plaque affixed on the side of the towering statue reads: "Biscuit's courage, honesty and physical prowess definitely place him among the thoroughbred immortals of turf history. He had intelligence and understanding almost spiritual in quality." Its location, almost directly across the street from the Saratoga Race Track, makes it one of the most popular (and most photographed) venues of the area.

Wheeler cast two identical statues of Seabiscuit. When Charles Howard died, one of them (the Saratoga one) was donated by his family to stand outside the entrance to the National Racing Museum and Hall of Fame. The champion horse himself unveiled the second one (by pulling a curtain open with his mouth) in February 1941 at the paddock area of Santa Anita Race Track in Arcadia, California, the scene of some of his most glorious victories. (A statue of jockey George Woolf stands nearby. It was also sculpted by Wheeler.)

Today, Popcorn Deelites is the star resident at Old Friend's Horse Rescue Farm in Georgetown, Kentucky. A new third replica of the famous Tex Wheeler statue of Seabiscuit was unveiled at the champion's grave at Ridgewood Ranch, in Willits, California, in 2007. As Tracy Livingston, president of the Seabiscuit Heritage Foundation, said, "It's good to have the Biscuit home."

WHILE HERE

They say that Saratoga is "the August place to be," and they are right. This city really gets "plugged in" during race month, and the streets and sidewalks swell with thousands of bettors, concertgoers, and tourists. The racetrack is a marvel of old Victorian architecture and just oozes with history and charm (tours are given). Much of the old downtown business district is unrecognizable from its turn-of-the-century quaintness, save for the building facades. The "malling of Saratoga" has taken place, and the downtown area, though enjoyable to walk and to window shop, is pretty much an outdoor shopping mall. Most of the major high-end chain stores are here, from Ann Taylor to the Gap to Talbot's. A number of independently owned stores along Broadway (the city's Main Street) sell unusual glass items, original art, souvenirs, and handcrafts. Many fine restaurants, bars, cafés, and ice cream parlors dot the business district landscape.

A saving grace for the downtown area is its immediate proximity to famous Congress Park, which opens onto Broadway. A stunningly beautiful public park, it contains bucolic walking paths; Italian Carrera marble statues, including the whimsical Spit and Spat Fountain, which features two cherubs spitting water at each other; an arboretum's worth of dazzling flowers and trees; and a working carousel. Constructed by Marcus Illions, this is a one-of-a-kind merry-go-round built on Coney Island; it is breathtaking in its beauty and kids from eight to eighty love to take a ride on it! The grand Canfield Casino is here, with its sweeping arches and original Tiffany stained glass windows, harking back to a day when gambling was the second most popular form of entertainment in the city (after the horses, of course!). It now houses the Saratoga Historical Society.

One of the most famous statues in Congress Park is the Spirit of Life, a regal winged Venus holding court at the end of a languid, marble rimmed reflection pool. It was created by Daniel Chester French in 1915; French is most famous for his statue of Abraham Lincoln at the Lincoln Memorial in Washington, DC. Many of the famous Saratoga springs themselves are in the park. These springs are covered with ornate marble edifices, yet invite the passerby to sample some of the heavily mineral-laden "cures" with names like the Columbian, the Congress, the Freshwater, the Hamilton, among others.

Clearly the jewel of Saratoga has to be the Adelphi Hotel at 365 Broadway. It is the essence of old Saratoga. Built in 1877, the structure literally sprawls the length of a half-city block in the heart of downtown. Its gracefulness, beauty, history, and lore are essential parts of modern-day Saratoga, acting both as a bridge to its storied past and as a present-day reminder of the powers of positive restoration for our vanishing historical treasures. A visit inside the Adelphi is like taking a gentle step through the looking glass and is a must-see for any visit to this fair city. In October 1997, *Heritage Magazine* gave out its initial Great American Place Award. It is without a doubt that the grandest lady of them all, the Adelphi Hotel, was a major reason why Saratoga Springs won this award!

One of the most popular off the beaten path destinations for Saratogians and the thousands of visitors that come here each year is the Parting Glass Pub (40 Lake Street; just few minutes' walk from Broadway). It is Saratoga's oldest and largest Irish bar and restaurant and features one of the nation's most active dart halls! Good food, traditional Irish music (live!), and a friendly wait staff make a visit here memorable.

A block from the Parting Glass, at 47 Phila Street, is Caffè Lena. Its unpretentious exterior (don't blink or you'll miss it!) belies the history of this upstairs coffeehouse. Founded by the legendary Lena Spencer in 1960 (making it the oldest coffeehouse in America), it continues on long after her death in 1989 as a nonprofit home for live music. The famed upstairs living room is tiny (it seats less than 100) and hot, but if the walls could talk, oh, what a story they would tell! From one of Bob Dylan's first performances to unforgettable appearances by Ani DiFranco, Arlo Guthrie, Don Maclean, Jerry Jeff Walker, Odetta, Emmylou Harris, Nanci Griffith, and many more, Caffè Lena is without a doubt one of America's most historic and seminal live music venues. No food or alcohol is allowed, but downstairs you will be glad to find Hattie's, a popular restaurant serving drinks and Southern/Cajun food for more than seven decades.

On a final note, huge wall-to-wall murals by famed artist Guy Pene du Bois, depicting Saratoga social scenes of the 1930s, can be enjoyed at the main Saratoga Post Office.

REFERENCE FILE

Although there are many books on the life of Seabiscuit, including Laura Hillenbrand's classic, there are many other lesser-known titles to consider while looking for a book on this champion. For an interesting take on this legendary horse, the reader can choose from many popular children's books. Seabiscuit was quite popular in his day, particularly with children. *Seabiscuit the Wonder Horse* by Meghan McCarthy (Simon and Schuster, 2008) is an excellent version of the horse's story skewed to the young reader.

Hughlette "Tex" Wheeler was a famous sculptor of Western themes. He did the iconic statue of Will Rogers that stands at Will Rogers State Park in Santa Monica, California. For his biography and photos of his work visit http://www.bronze-gallery.com.

SYRACUSE'S FINEST HOUR

The Jerry Rescue Monument, Syracuse

Syracuse, New York, is centrally located in the state and is the engine that basically drives the Central New York economy. A city of about 140,000 people, Syracuse, like its upstate neighbors, has been steadily losing residents for a half-century (the population in 1950 was 240,000). At both a natural and symbolic crossroads of the region, Syracuse has been the economic hub, a seat of higher education, and a major trading destination ever since the Onondaga Nation, a member tribe of the Iroquois Confederacy, invited French missionaries to establish a trading post here in the 1600s. The mission lasted only a couple of years, but the roots of progress were planted and nurtured until more permanent settlers arrived after the Revolutionary War.

Huge deposits of salt were discovered along Syracuse's five-mile long lake, Onondaga Lake, and that brought even more settlers and businesses. In 1848, the Erie Canal was routed through Syracuse, bringing a boomtown atmosphere to this once-sleepy community. As farmers moved more and more pork along the canal route (pork that needed to be salt-cured), the salt industry swelled to become the number one business in Syracuse. The city's official nickname was (and some think, still is) the Salt City, and by 1850, it was the twelfth largest city in the country. Unfortunately, Onondaga Lake is today a major embarrassment for Syracuse. Decades of industrial dumping have left it barren and in a state of ecological rigor mortis. It has been called the most polluted body of water in the world. That said, the city is in an ever-ongoing process of rehabilitating the lake with some small measures of success.

Today, Syracuse seems to be turning a corner, both aesthetically and financially. While all of Upstate New York absorbs the continuous and devastating blows of a sluggish economy and a flight of taxpayers, the city does have some bright spots that seem to be spearheading a more positive outlook for the coming years. Syracuse University is a prominent US college and the major employer in the region (6,800 employees). Upstate Medical University and Hospital (with 6,500 employees) is right behind it.

Syracuse University is home to nearly nineteen thousand students from around the world who come here to major in business, science, architecture, and communications. The college originated the field of journalistic studies, and its S. I. Newhouse School of Public Communications (established in 1934) is considered one of the best of its kind in the world. It boasts a roster of graduates such as Bob Costas, Ted Koppel, Dick Clark, Marv Albert, and many others.

The Orangemen and Orangewomen have fielded legendary teams in various Division I sports for decades. Many of the school's teams play at the Carrier Dome, named after the once-thriving Carrier Air Conditioning Company, based in Syracuse. The fifty-thousand-seat dome is the largest domed stadium in the East.

The New York State Fair has been hosting generations of fun lovers at its permanent home in Syracuse since 1860. It is the largest and oldest state fair in America. Nearly one million New Yorkers flood the fairgrounds at the end of each summer to catch national entertainers, thrill in the old fashioned carnival midway, and eat their way through a mile-long food court featuring such New York originals as hot wings (Buffalo), chicken riggies (Utica), and spiedies (Binghamton).

THE MONUMENT

Syracuse has always had one of the largest proportions of black residents of any city in New York. Before the Civil War it was one of the most important Underground Railroad stations in the North, and the city was peopled with and visited by the greatest names of the abolitionist movement (antislavery leader Gerrit Smith lived in nearby Peterboro, Harriet Tubman lived in nearby Auburn, and Frederick Douglass and Susan B. Anthony were from neighboring Rochester). Syracuse was a feisty bastion of abolitionist passions in the pre–Civil War days, and one event in particular showcased the city's pride in self-determination, rebellious nature toward outside influence, and deeply held libertarian principles not found in many of the communities of the time. That singular event is known as the Jerry Rescue.

On September 18, 1850, Congress enacted the Fugitive Slave Law. The nonslave North hated this new mandate, which basically called upon all free-thinking northerners to act as a "police force" for the South. As more and more slaves fled their shackles to the freedom of the northern states, the new law now demanded that every law officer in the North aggressively act to find those fugitives and return them, by force, to their owners in the South. Many believe that the Fugitive Slave Law was the match that lit the flame that caused the firestorm of civil war to break out a decade later.

In Syracuse, the heart of antislave New York, the act was met with derision and open defiance. Local leaders declared their city "free to all men," and fugitives poured in from the South, coming as both permanent residents of the city or passengers on the Underground Railroad to points north (Canada). The US secretary of state at the time, the esteemed Daniel Webster, a much-hated man here for his support of the law, hurled an oratorical bomb at the opponents of this law, particularly the independent-minded citizens of Syracuse. In May 1851, Webster went to Syracuse to demand a stop to the insurgent acts actively thwarting the fugitive law in the city. In a fiery speech to a crowd near the balcony of the Syracuse City Hall, the secretary of state, known as one of the greatest public speakers of his time, laid down the gauntlet. "The Fugitive Slave Law *will* be executed in all the great cities, *including* here in Syracuse, and *even* during the upcoming Anti-Slave Convention if the occasion shall arise!" he thundered.

William "Jerry" Henry, a free black citizen of Syracuse, was at work as a barrel maker when on October 1, 1851, a large posse arrested him at his place of employment for theft. He was shackled and led away. Only when he was safely behind bars did the arresting officers reveal that he was actually being held for being an escaped slave and his return to his southern owner was imminent. In an eerie prophecy of Daniel Webster's threat, the Anti-Slavery Convention was in fact being held in Syracuse at that very time. Word of Jerry's arrest raced through the streets of Syracuse right to the floor of the convention. The members surged into the streets and marched to the building where he was being held.

The mob, both black and white, created an uproar for the officers guarding their prisoner. Samuel Ward, an ex-slave and one of the most prominent abolitionist leaders in the country, took to the speaker's box. The crowd went silent.

"We are witnessing such a sight I pray we may never see again. Look! Look!" he roared. "A man in chains . . . *here in Syracuse!*"

With that, a roar went up from the throng, church bells began to peal across the city, and an altercation broke out. In the confusion, William "Jerry" Henry escaped, though still in manacles. He was quickly recaptured and secured by the police. The mob promised to return the next night and complete their rescue.

The following evening, a crowd of more than two thousand converged on the jail. Armed guards took position from inside the building, but they were no match for the fury of the angry Syracusans. Gunshots were fired, a deputy was injured while falling from a window, a battering ram was produced, and the crowd, black and white, young and old, men and women, beat down the front door and flooded the building. Once inside they freed the prisoner and hurried him out amid the raucous commotion of the riot. Jerry was taken to the home of a sympathetic butcher where he hid for several days before arrangements were made to book him passage on the Underground Railroad into Canada, and freedom.

This daring act, the boldest uprising of good against evil by ordinary citizens at the time, was heralded in the press nationwide and fanned the flames on both sides of the slavery issue. Nineteen citizens of Syracuse were arrested for their role in the Jerry Rescue, but they were freed after the former governor of New York, William Seward, personally signed their bail bond! Of the nineteen, none served jail time.

The courage of the good people of Syracuse is memorialized today with the Jerry Rescue Monument in Clinton Square, downtown Syracuse. The twelve-foot-tall bronze, brick, and granite sculpture is a tableau of fear and determination, and the image of the rescued man emerging three-dimensionally from his "prison" is heart stopping. The sculptor, Sharon BuMann, of Central Square, New York, has perfectly captured the moment of that unforgettable October night in 1851. Officially, the monument is known as the Jerry Rescue Abolitionist Monument. The symbolism of the memorial, from the four-pointed star base to the red warehouse bricks used in the construction, is described on a plaque affixed to one of the walls. Another plaque tells the story of the rescue itself.

BuMann creates a work of immediacy and danger in this memorial and includes two other important figures along with Jerry. The two figures hustling the frightened slave to freedom are Rev. Samuel May and Rev. Jermain Logan, two area clergymen involved in the local Underground Railroad.

Sadly, all of the original buildings that played a part in the Jerry Rescue are now long gone, victims of urban sprawl. The historic building where the prisoner was jailed and, ultimately, freed, is now a parking lot. The monument is all that is left in preserving what many have called Syracuse's finest hour. A descriptive plaque across the street shows a period map of the area and denotes where the key places of the event took place.

WHILE HERE

There are great similarities among the larger, older cities of Upstate New York. Forgotten, less vigorous downtowns, sprawling suburbs, great shopping malls on the outskirts of town, turn-of-the-century architecture, and a civic pride that endeavors to retain and revitalize as much of the good old days as possible (against formidable odds) are all the hallmarks of the region. The scene is repeated across the state, from Utica to Rochester to Binghamton to Schenectady to Kingston. Syracuse, benefiting from a large segment of young and vital residents (Syracuse University) as well as a large population of highly trained, highly paid medical professionals, seems to be faring better than some of its upstate brethren. Syracuse lacks in a lot of leisurely, "touristy" things to do (in the city proper) but it does boast an energy and ebullience that is palpable, even in the struggling downtown areas. There are two fun and highly unusual "monuments" to visit in the city, monuments that you will definitely *not* see the likes of anywhere else.

Clinton Square, in the heart of downtown Syracuse, is a revitalized area of pubs, restaurants, and festival locations, much like it was in the 1870s, when a local brewer hosted a "festival of the poor" that attracted as many as twenty thousand revelers. Now, concerts, street theater, and emerging retail venues are the hallmark of this historic center of Syracuse. Clinton Square is a dynamic central location. A sprawling outdoor area for lunchtime crowds to gather or for weekend sun worshippers to bask in the few sunny days a year experienced in Syracuse, the square is an integral part of Syracuse's economic turnaround. And the history here, still very much preserved, is awesome. Some newer buildings, such as the Syracuse Post-Standard Newspaper Building and the Atrium at Clinton Square are located here, but the emphasis of the square is old and historic!

The center of the square is cleaved by a wide stretch that was actually where the Erie Canal ran through the downtown business district (now used as a winter skating rink). On one side is the towering Soldiers and Sailors Monument. This behemoth was dedicated before fifty thousand Syracusans on June 21, 1910, with the official declaration read by Vice President James S. Sherman. A century later, the magnificently restored monument (which pays tribute to Syracuse's 149th Company B Civil War troops) was rededicated with a huge throng in attendance, including the great-grandnephew of Mr. Sherman. One of the large bronze bas reliefs, on the western side, is titled Mending the Flag and depicts a local Syracuse young man, Sgt. Lilly, mending the company's shattered flag at Culp's Hill at the Battle of Gettysburg.

In the background of Clinton Square, you can see a chorus line of the grand dames of Syracuse's architecture: the Third National Bank (1886), Syracuse Savings Bank (1876), the Gridley Building (1867), and the Onondaga Savings Bank (1897). They are all in beautifully restored condition and ring the square.

Tipperary Hill, on Syracuse's far west side, is an Irish enclave that traces its roots back nearly two centuries. The Irish had made up the majority of the muscle that built the Erie Canal through here, and when it was completed they settled in this hillside neighborhood overlooking their handiwork.

Syracuse began installing its hanging traffic lights in the beginning of the 1920s. At the time these were quite the curiosity. When one was placed on Tipperary Hill (Tompkins Street at Milton Avenue), many of the residents came out to marvel at this safety advancement. Some of the Irish lads, however, did not take kindly to the sequence of the colored lamps, with red on top, yellow in the middle, and green on the bottom. They contrived that the red on top insinuated British over Irish, and a great sport came about of hurling rocks and smashing the red lamps out of the traffic lights. Week after week the transportation workers of the city of Syracuse would come to Tipp Hill and replace the broken lamps, only to have the new ones destroyed shortly after they left. Soon, the city threw up its hands and caved to the neighborhood. The result? The crossing light at Tipperary Hill in Syracuse is the only place *in the nation* where you will find the hanging lamp with the light sequence inverted: red on the bottom and green on the top. A small park sits at the intersection with a statue commemorating this "Irish victory." The monument depicts a young girl, a man (pointing to the hanging lamp), and a young Irish lad with a slingshot about to let it fly. The sculptor is Dexter Benedict, of Penn Yan, New York. In Syracuse, every St. Patrick's Day begins with the painting over of the white line down the middle of the highway under the Tipp Hill light with a Kelly green. On March 15, 2005, Irish Prime Minister Bertie Ahern came to Tipperary Hill to see the light for himself!

The Shot Clock Monument is without a doubt one of the most unusual commemorations this writer has ever seen. Located on the sidewalk in the busy Armory Square district of downtown Syracuse, the monument is, well, just that . . . a basketball twenty-four-second shot clock! Why?

Basketball had been losing momentum and fans during the 1950s, and Coach Howard Hobson (Oregon and Yale) and Danny Biasone, owner of the NBA's Syracuse Nationals, came up with the idea of a countdown clock that forced players to throw the ball up, instead of the endless clock-killing passes of the decade before, which bored the crowds and made for some very low-scoring games. Biasone divided 2,880 (the number of seconds in a regulation NBA game) by 120 (the number of shots taken at the time in a normal game) to come up with the arbitrary number of twenty-four seconds. He convinced the NBA to adopt this clock in 1955, the same year his Syracuse Nats won the championship.

On March 26, 2005, the Shot Clock Monument was unveiled to a crowd of hundreds in Armory Square (among those attending were the surviving members of the 1955 champion Syracuse Nationals). The giant replica of the shot clock actually works, is lit up, and is perpetually counting down twenty-four seconds to the passersby, tourists, and shoppers walking beneath it. It is adorned with a large plaque telling of its creation and the Syracuse connection to it.

This monument to sports innovation has been featured in *Sports Illustrated,* television's *Wide World of Sports,* and many other national media outlets. It is 25 percent larger than the original shot clock was. The original is housed at LeMoyne College in Syracuse.

The Erie Canal Museum is located at 318 Erie Boulevard East, just two short city blocks from the Jerry Rescue Monument. This museum tells the compelling story of the building of the Erie Canal, the greatest engineering marvel of its day. Out front, right on the sidewalk, is a wonderful statue of a young boy and his mule. This is the famous "Mule Named Sal" of the famous folk song by Thomas Allen ("I've got an old mule and her name is Sal; fifteen miles on the Erie Canal"). The importance of these reliable beasts of burden in the success of the canal cannot be understated, and it is well worth a five-minute walk to this site for a photo or a pat on the rump of this statue to say thanks to the unsung hero of the Erie Canal.

Go another five-minute walk in a different direction from Clinton Square and you will come upon another legendary Syracuse icon. The Dinosaur Bar-B-Que restaurant, at 246 Willow Street, is a rough-hewn, bike-strewn, leather and tat rib joint that has been called America's finest barbecue stand outside of the South! The waitresses are gritty, the walls are grafittied, the ribs are greasy, and the smell is the closest thing to heaven you will find in any eatery in Upstate New York. Put your waitin' shoes on as crowds pack this place all day long, but the wait is well worth it. And the corn bread and beans on the side will make you wish you could take it all home with you (and you can by visiting their popular online store at http://www.dinosaurbarbeque.com).

REFERENCE FILE

There are many books about the history of Syracuse, but one of the nicest (and priciest) is a gorgeous coffee table book titled *Historic Photos of Syracuse* by Dennis Connors (Turner Publishing, 2008). This 216-page book is filled with lush archival photos of Syracuse, including the historic Erie Canal crossing at Clinton Square where the Jerry Rescue Memorial is now located. Connors is the curator of history for the Onondaga Historical Association.

Sharon BuMann is a noted New York sculptor with many examples of her work on display in the Syracuse/Central New York region. Her Jerry Rescue memorial is her signature work. For images of BuMann's work, including her many popular state fair butter sculptures, visit her Web site at http://www.sharon bumann.com.

THE SPIRIT OF AMERICA

The Uncle Sam Memorial, Troy

Troy, New York, is the third sister in the Capital District's family, situated on the eastern shore of the Hudson River, across from its "siblings," nearby Albany and the farther west Schenectady.

Troy (named after Homer's city in the *Iliad*) has a population of fewer than 50,000 and has refashioned itself over the years from a city of iron to a city of ideas. Troy was one of the great original American iron centers in the beginning of the nineteenth century. In fact, located here was the first American Bessemer converter, a revolutionary process that dramatically shortened the time in turning raw pig iron into steel. Troy iron and steel, arriving from the west via the newly opened Erie Canal (the city is just east of Albany, the eastern terminus of Clinton's Ditch), was processed here and then sent down river to form the great edifices of New York City. After the Civil War, good fortunes continued for Troy even as the iron industry slowly moved west. By the end of the nineteenth century it was one of the most prosperous cities in the nation. Mansions and carriage houses dotted the landscapes of the rich and famous citizens of Troy. The list of millionaires grew as new commerce began to flourish on the eastern banks of the Hudson River. Universities, financial institutions, department stores, and river excursion companies all sprung up with increasing degrees of success. Troy continued to prosper into the first quarter of the twentieth century. But it was the simple shirt collar that really put Troy on the map!

In 1827, Troy resident Hannah Montague grew frustratingly tired of washing her laborer husband's white shirt collar every day despite the fact that the shirt proper remained unsoiled. "Ring around the collar" was really causing Hannah

a "pain in the neck!" One day she patched together a removable collar out of a single piece of cloth and a couple of buttons and off her husband, Orlando, went to work. The next day, she simply replaced the collar with a new clean one, on the same shirt.

By the early twentieth century, there were hundreds of workers employed by the more than two dozen shirt and collar makers in Troy (by now it was officially called Collar City). Nine out of every ten shirt collars in America were made in this city. Even more fortunes were made. A clean white collar became increasingly important as a middle level of management began to develop between labor and owners, and Troy's collar industry led to the term "white collar worker."

Like Albany, its big sister across the river, Troy is home to a disproportionate number of excellent, storied seats of learning. Rensselaer Polytechnic Institute, one of the great universities in the world, was founded in 1824 and hosts sixty-five hundred students (including many international students) on its sprawling 275-acre campus. It is one of the wealthiest colleges in Upstate New York, with an endowment of over $700 million.

Russell Sage College, founded as a women's college by a suffragist leader in 1916, enrolls approximately one thousand students yearly in its classes, which are held in a multitude of fabulous old Victorian buildings and homes around the campus. Russell Sage College was founded and funded by Margaret Olivia Slocum, widow of infamous Wall Street tightwad Russell Sage. That the late Mr. Sage thought education for women was frivolous and a complete waste of time and money must have been a source of great amusement for his progressive and beneficent widow. The beauty of the Russell Sage campus has been seen by millions, on screen. Among the films shot on campus is Martin Scorcese's 1993 adaptation of Edith Wharton's classic, *The Age of Innocence*, starring Daniel Day-Lewis.

For a small school (approximately three hundred students, attended by fifty teachers), Emma Willard holds a large endowment of nearly $100 million (Jane Fonda, class of 1955, is a generous alumna). And, not to be outdone, the stunning architecture of the Emma Willard campus can be seen in full Technicolor glory in the 2002 Kevin Kline film *The Emperor's Club* as well as the 1992 Academy Award–winning *The Scent of a Woman*, starring Al Pacino. Oddly, both Hollywood depictions of this women's institution were that of boys' schools!

THE MONUMENT

Samuel Wilson, a Troy meatpacker, used to stamp his provision barrels with the initials "US" before shipping his meat out to the troops during the War of 1812. Apocryphal as it might be, many believe to this day that Sam Wilson is the nexus of the image of America we know today as Uncle Sam (his employees referred to the US-branded barrels as "Uncle Sam's meat"). From one generation to another, the Uncle Sam legend and legacy grew until it landed in the lap of the famed illustrator James Montgomery Flagg. On July 6, 1916, Flagg's iconic Uncle Sam made his debut on the cover of the popular *Leslie's Weekly Magazine*, red, white, and blue top hat, rolled up sleeves, wispy white beard, and all (none of which Samuel Wilson wore). This became the famous "I Want You!" wartime poster, and between 1917 and 1919 more than four million posters were sold. The image was solidified in the minds of nearly every American.

Samuel Wilson was an upstanding citizen of Troy remembered more for his cultural image than for his meatpacking skills. In the latter part of the twentieth century, Troy's city fathers finally came to the realization that "the Home of Uncle Sam" had a far more Chamber of Commerce–friendly sound to it than "the Home of the Detachable Collar," and the city's identity was forever changed. Uncle Sam images flourish on every neighborhood street corner, upon every imaginable type of business ("Uncle Sam's Original Pizza"), and on street signs and park memorials throughout. Samuel Wilson's grave, in Oakwood Cemetery, is one of the most visited sights in the area, and a local Boy Scout troop raises and lowers an American flag over his grave every day.

The Uncle Sam Monument stands in Riverfront Park, along the Hudson River in downtown Troy. It is at the junction of three major city roads: River, Fulton, and Third Streets. A generous slice of green amid this bustling pedestrian area, the park offers leafy refuge for visitors, office workers, and transients alike (a major bus drop-off location and the city's municipal parking garage adjoin the park). The statue is a brilliant, gleaming stainless steel-looking depiction of Uncle Sam in full regalia. In a subtle nod to the stylings of Frank Gehry, the monument seems to defy traditional form and figure and instead takes on a much more fluid, kinetic shape. Uncle Sam's cape seems to billow before you, his hair seems to wave in the gentle river breeze, and his withering gaze telegraphs that this is a man (read: country) not to mess around with!

Dedicated in 1980, the citation at the base of the giant statue reads:

Troy's Citizen, and America's Uncle! The big thing is not what happens to us in life, but rather what we *do* about what happens to us in life. Samuel Wilson.

The sculptor, K. George Kratina, created, much like Flagg did nearly one hundred years ago, an Uncle Sam for the new century.

The park also has two other notable sculptures worth seeing while visiting Uncle Sam. Directly behind the statue is a tall pillar with a magnificent bronze bust on it, erected in 1986. Irish patriot and martyr James Connolly, who lived briefly in Troy, is memorialized here. Connolly was a founder of the Irish Citizens Army and was executed in Ireland for his role in the famous Easter Uprising. During the rebellion Connolly was gravely wounded. On May 12, 1916, despite the severity of his injuries, he was dragged from his prison cell, tied to a chair, and executed. Today, he is revered throughout Scotland, the land of his birth, and Ireland. The sculptor, Paula O'Sullivan, included this chilling Connolly uprising quote on the monument: "Be men now, or be forever slaves!"

Anchoring the far end of the park is the Troy Vietnam Memorial. The haunting sculpture, created by Eileen Barry in 1991, is poignant and powerful in its harrowing depiction of three US soldiers in the heat of battle in the jungles of Southeast Asia. The memorial, entitled Courage Compassion Pain, is to honor (in the sculptor's own words) "the soldiers and not the war."

Just three blocks from this park is the Rensselaer County Soldiers and Sailors Monument, at Broadway and Second Streets. This is the heart of "Old Troy." The monument has been called one of the most impressive war memorials in the nation. Designed by Caspar Buberl (who created more than a dozen Civil War monuments at the Gettysburg Battlefield) and erected in what was then Washington Park on September 15, 1891, the shaft of this inspiring memorial soars nearly one hundred feet in the air, making it one of Troy's most striking landmarks (and its de facto logo). The park's name was changed to Monument Park at the dedication ceremony of the memorial. A salute to Troy's veterans of several wars, it features several bronze bas relief depictions of battle scenes, which skirt the base of the monument and tell the story of the more than one hundred fifty major battles fought by Trojans in the nineteenth century. Included in these battles is the great Battle of the Ironclads during the

Civil War. The panel depicts the USS Monitor battling the Confederate ship Merrimack. Much of the framework of the USS Monitor was made in the iron foundries of Troy.

WHILE HERE

Monument Park well points you on a walking tour of Troy, which includes River Street, home to a popular annual antique street festival. Among the many antique shops, cafés, bookstores, and art galleries is one of the most interesting buildings on the street, at 225 River Street (once the home of Troy's leading newspaper, *The Troy Sentinel*). A plaque on the front wall reads, "T'was the night before Christmas when all thro' the house / Not a creature was stirring, not even a mouse . . . Written in 1822 by Dr. Clement C. Moore for his children and first published on this site." A chiseled legend on this same building darkly remembers that "The destructive fire of June 20, 1820, was arrested here." That fire, a million dollar fire, nearly destroyed the entire city of Troy.

Four blocks south of Monument Park is the urban campus of Russell Sage College. This historic seat of learning consists of many great buildings and memorials. Entering the campus at Robison Court (Congress and Second Streets), one is confronted with a large, magnificent statue of Emma Hart Willard, a pioneer in women's education in America. The intricate Victorian detail on the statue is truly amazing, from the dainty silk cuffs on her sleeves to the decorative tassels on the chair on which she sits. It is a wondrous piece of public art. Created by Alexander Doyle in 1895, the plaque reminds us that this is "the site of America's first women's college, 1821." The statue was completely restored in 2001 and is in pristine condition.

While visiting the Russell Sage campus, be sure and go to the Julia Howard Bush Memorial Center, just a hundred paces into the campus from the Willard statue. This replica of the Greek Parthenon is open to the general public and is gorgeous. Designed by prolific architect James Harrison, this is one of only ten examples of his work left in the United States. The interior is a stunning display of Greek-themed nuances (domed ceilings, columns, and so on) and modern accouterments (such as indirect lighting, public address systems). The walls are lined with towering, ancient stained-glass windows, three of them signed by Louis Comfort Tiffany himself!

For a fun side trip, only a few blocks south of the center of the business district and at the edge of the newly revitalized Little Italy section of the city, travel a short distance out to 280 4th Street. If you stop and observe the neighborhood, it might just look familiar to you.

The famed Americana artist Norman Rockwell was a frequent visitor to Troy, and he used some of the people and locations as inspirations for his paintings. One such painting, *The Street Was Never the Same Again,* depicts the ruckus caused when the first automobile sputters down a city street. In the image, a well-dressed driver steers his "horseless carriage" down a crowded city street as neighbors and passersby gaze upon him wide-eyed and startled at the new fangled contraption. Little children run along next to the car shouting in glee, horses rear up in fright, and people lean far out of every window to catch a glimpse of the life-changing invention debuting on their very own street. The painting, commissioned by the Ford Motor Company in 1952, is one of Rockwell's most beloved works. A New York State historical marker here informs the visitor that this is the block and buildings used as models for the painting (and yes, they remain unchanged after over a half century!).

REFERENCE FILE

Troy has embraced the Uncle Sam mystique with a warm and enveloping hug. The statue to Uncle Sam in the riverside park is only one of many tributes to this symbol of Americana in the city. To learn more about Uncle Sam and many other American icons, read the fun children's book *Uncle Sam and Old Glory: Symbols of America* by Delno C. West and Jean M. West (Atheneum, 2000). Keeping Uncle Sam company in this light-hearted book are Smokey the Bear, the Statue of Liberty, the American buffalo, the bald eagle, Yankee Doodle Dandy, and many more.

Brooklyn-born sculptor's George Kratina's work can be found throughout the nation. Another great piece is Singing Thanksgiving, a moving tribute to the founders of our nation. This giant statue stands in the York (Pennsylvania) Post Office. To view this creation visit http://www.yorkblog.com.

OLD KINDERHOOK

The Van Buren Statue, Kinderhook

One of my favorite regions of Upstate New York is that little slice of heaven that runs between the Hudson River and the borders of the New England states. Encompassing Washington, Rensselaer, Columbia, Dutchess, and Putnam counties, it is an area steeped in beauty and history that is still (for the most part) a secret place unaffected by the encroachments of urban flight. At most, the widest stretch of this region is an hour's drive from the river to the state line, but oh what that hour's drive beholds. Some of the quaintest and oldest villages and towns in the state are here, reflecting Revolutionary War history, Old Dutch heritage, magnificent horse farms, Shaker religion influences, folk heroes and folk legends (including the Headless Horseman!), rural life as depicted by the slice of heaven resident Grandma Moses, apple orchards as far as the eye can see, and unforgettable Thomas Cole vistas of the stunning Hudson, "America's First River."

A whole panorama of American history is played out along this 150-mile strip of the Empire State: painter Frederick Church's aerie known as Olana; FDR's beloved Hyde Park home, where he was born and is buried; Vassar College and Rensselaer Polytechnic Institute, two of our nation's finest universities; Locust Grove, the home of Samuel F. B. Morse; Sing Sing Prison, the infamous jail where criminals first went "up the river to the big house"; the Culinary Institute of America, one of the world's premier culinary colleges; the Beekman Arms Hotel, the nation's oldest inn; the Old Rhinebeck Aerodrome, the nation's oldest aviation museum; and much more. Truly, this slice of heaven is one of New York's greatest treasures.

171

Kinderhook is nestled in this area, in Columbia County, just a few short miles from the banks of the Hudson River. Legend has it that Henry Hudson, on his maiden voyage up the Hudson River, moored his ship, the *Half Moon*, at the present site of the village and noticed a large number of Indian (Mohican) children gathering and waving from the shoreline. Hence the Dutch name Kinderhook, which means "children's corner."

The town's 8,500 residents enjoy the beauty and seclusion of the Hudson Valley while also having the luxury of being nearby to larger cities (Albany, for example, with its international airport and access to Amtrak and the NYS Thruway, is very close). This is farm country, with miles of well-tended dairy farms, endless acres of apple orchards, and farm markets at every crossroads. Some of the oldest homes of the Hudson Valley are located here, including, in a neighboring village, the famous Livingston family estate, Clermont. This five-hundred-acre country manse was home to several generations of the Livingston family. Robert

R. Livingston Jr. (1746–1813) was an original signer of the Declaration of Independence, served as our nation's first secretary of state, and gave the oath of office to George Washington when he was sworn in as president. He also partnered with Robert Fulton in building the *North River,* the first steamboat to traverse the Hudson River (a ship that many people incorrectly identify today as the *Clermont*). The home is open to the public and features several buildings and lavish gardens, a visitor's center, and a research area. Many thousands visit Clermont each year, and it is heralded as one of the greatest of the Hudson Mansions.

While Clermont is a few minutes drive from Kinderhook (in a town that is the same as the mansion), there are plenty of historical sights in the village of Kinderhook itself to please the curious weekend warrior. Not the least is Lindenwald, the home and farm of our nation's eighth president, Martin Van Buren. Also in town are the Luykas Van Alen House (built in 1737), the James Vanderpoel House (c. 1820), and the Ichabod Crane Schoolhouse (c. 1850). The latter (moved to the grounds of the Van Alen House in 1974) was the place of employment for Jesse Merwin. Merwin was the headmaster at this small country school in the mid-1800s, when Washington Irving was a frequent visitor to the area. Irving is said to have patterned his character, the schoolteacher Ichabod Crane, after Merwin in his classic *The Legend of Sleepy Hollow.* All of these buildings are restored and open to the public, and all are within close proximity, lined right up along Kinderhook's main street, NYS Route 9.

A little further north of Kinderhook is the lavish estate of artist Frederic Church, Olana. This Persian-style home, a mountaintop confection of sweeping Hudson River vistas, whimsical architectural flourishes, winding dirt roads, and secret walking paths, is a classic example of the many Hudson Valley restored mansions that are open to the public. Having said this, there is nothing typical about Church's grand sweeping mish-mash of architectural odds and ends that make Olana so intriguing (note the teapots on top of the tallest tower of the house).

Kinderhook is today a wealthy, prosperous little country village, with beautiful homes, a charming business district, and wide tree-shaded roads. Even nearly 150 years ago, when its most famous citizen walked the streets of town, it was a place of commerce, culture, and country charm. That citizen was Martin Van Buren, and his statuary memorial is the most recently dedicated monument in this book.

THE STATUE

Martin Van Buren was the first president born in the United States (think about it for a minute and you will understand!). Being of Dutch descent, Van Buren was the only president to whom English was a *second* language (he and his parents spoke only Dutch in their home). A diminutive figure in real life (5 feet 6 inches), he was an icon who cast a long shadow throughout the Hudson Valley region of his birth. Basically credited with creating the modern-day Democratic Party as we know it, Van Buren helmed the Albany Regency, one of the most effective and powerful political bases in the country. He even served one term as New York governor. Known locally as "Old Kinderhook," the Dutchman was the focus of "OK" clubs throughout the state, giving his supporters a grass roots home to organize in his name (in fact, the OK clubs were the first known reference of the usage of "OK" to describe something as satisfactory). He was elected to the US Senate in 1821, where the press dubbed him "the Little Magician" for his adroit handling of sticky political situations. Andrew Jackson tagged him to run with him as vice president in the presidential election of 1832. They won, and Van Buren succeeded his mentor as the eighth president of the United States in 1837.

After his single term of office ended, he retired to his elegant mansion, Lindenwald, in Kinderhook, where he continued to plan an unfulfilled return to the White House. He died in his bed on July 24, 1862. He is buried in the village cemetery.

Van Buren was the first of many firsts: He was the first president to marry a relative (he wed his cousin, Hannah Hoes, in 1807); he was the first president to enter the White House without a first lady (Hannah died at the age of thirty-five, before her husband was elected president. He remained a bachelor the rest of his life, and in fact never spoke of Hannah again, not even mentioning her in his autobiography!); and he was the first president who did not employ English as his first language. He was also the first New York State governor to be elected president. Others would follow though, including Grover Cleveland, Theodore Roosevelt, and Franklin Roosevelt. Thomas E. Dewey *almost* got elected president in 1948, and Governor Nelson Rockefeller served as Gerald Ford's vice president.

Surprisingly, the statues, monuments, and memorials to this beloved son of Kinderhook are few and far between; some might even say they are nonexistent. Lindenwald, the president's home, is under the care and guidance of the National Park Service and is a splendid home filled with many period pieces and artifacts of the Van Buren era. The Little Magician's final resting place in Kinderhook Cemetery is well pointed with signs and markers, and the grave itself is unmistakable. A large obelisk (the tallest in the cemetery) marks his grave and is visible from the road. A blue and orange New York State historical marker is street side to alert the passerby to this famous place. (Tourists to this tiny village will be pleased to find a multidirectional sign in the heart of the small business district pointing the way to the different Van Buren sites).

But where are the statues?

Well, there is finally a new statue in his honor right smack dab in the middle of the village green. In fact, it is so new that this tribute is the most recently placed of all the entries featured in *Monumental New York!* It was dedicated in front of the village bandstand gazebo at 2:00 p.m. on Saturday, July 14, 2007.

It is a wonderful tribute to the village's native son. Van Buren's famous bushy sideburns sprout out of the sides of his smiling face. His outfit is as refined in bronze as it was in life (he has been voted as the most well dressed and fastidious of all of our presidents). A fur-collared coat, with fur cuffs, covers a three-buttoned vest. His ubiquitous walking cane juts out with purpose from his right hand. His left hand holds a newspaper. The statue begs the viewer to approach and join the president on the period bronze park bench. Van Buren appears to be gazing across the street (NYS Route 9) at the Judge James Vanderpoel House, a 1820s mansion that is undergoing restoration. The restoration architect Doug Bucher called it "the ultimate example of Federal architecture in the Hudson Valley," and it is officially referred to as the House of History.

The sculptor is Edward Hlavka. There is an interesting story behind his statue of Van Buren.

The home of Mount Rushmore, Rapid City, South Dakota, wanted to honor even more presidents than the four depicted by Gutzon Borglum on the face of the Black Hills mountains (Washington, Lincoln, Jefferson, and Theodore Roosevelt). In 1997, the city decided that they would honor *all* of the US presidents with life-sized bronze statues of each scattered about the downtown business district. Each statue would have a benefactor, sometimes a Rapid City business or group or sometimes a supporter of a certain president (sponsorships cost $50,000). Each year four presidents would be chosen (two "older ones" and two "newer ones") until all were represented in 2011, as they worked toward the middle of the line of presidents.

Four native sculptors were chosen to create these presidential monuments, and Edward Hlavka, from Sturgis, South Dakota, was one of them. Each president is required to be depicted in "the style or manner of the period." President John F. Kennedy walks with young son John-John, Reagan strolls along in jeans and a cowboy hat, George Bush Sr. examines a world globe, Ike stands purposely in his military fatigues, Jimmy Carter is coatless, Nixon broods in an armchair, John Quincy Adams doffs his silk top hat, Gerald Ford carries his pipe, and the Little Magician sits on a park bench reading the *Kinderhook Rough Notes*, his hometown newspaper! One of the most popular statues is that of President Harry Truman. His image recreates the famous photo of him holding up a newspaper, which has an erroneous headline reading "Dewey Defeats Truman."

Sculptor Hlavka is responsible for the statues of Van Buren, Bush Sr., Nixon, and Jefferson. The Village of Kinderhook paid the "City of Presidents" (and Hlavka) $75,000 to have this statue recast and placed in their Columbia County community.

WHILE HERE

Kinderhook is a perfect jumping off place for day trips and afternoon drives. Albany is just a half hour away, as is southern Vermont and western Massachusetts. The Hudson River offers all sorts of leisurely activities, from boating to hiking to fishing. The many famous Hudson River mansions are all within an hour's drive, and it is very convenient to include a second president, Franklin D. Roosevelt, in your "history tour" of this region. Hyde Park is one of the most visited presidential homes in America; Lindenwald one of the least. Both, however, offer a heaping serving of Hudson Valley hospitality and history.

Just one hour south of Kinderhook on NYS Route 9 is FDR's home. In fact, Martin Van Buren's Lindenwald, is also on NYS Route 9. You might say that FDR and MVB were neighbors who lived just down the road from each other!

REFERENCE FILE

An excellent biography of the Little Magician is *Martin Van Buren: The Romantic Age of American Politics* by John Niven and Katherine Speirs (American Political Biography Press, 2000).

To see all of the presidential statues in the City of the Presidents go to http://www.visitrapidcity.com. To see other major works by sculptor Edward Hlavka, his Web site displays slide shows and still images of his commissions. It is at http://www.hlavka.com.

29

A TRIBUTE TO CANINE COURAGE

The War Dog Memorial, Hartsdale

Hartsdale, New York, is located in Westchester County, so to many (including me) it really doesn't qualify as Upstate New York, but it *is* just a few minutes from the Tappan Zee Bridge (my own arbitrary southern border of the area I call "Upstate"), it *is* just a few miles down the road from Putnam County where there are a couple of entries in this book, and it *does* have one of the most interesting statues, monuments, and memorials I have discovered. So, despite the fact that this particular road trip puts us a perilous thirty miles north of metropolitan New York it is certainly worth an entry in *Monumental New York!*

With a population of under 10,000 residents, Hartsdale is one of the smaller bedroom communities to New York City. The town now bustles with incoming and outgoing Metro North commuter trains and cross-county express roads, but it wasn't that long ago that the area (named after Robert Hart, a successful nineteenth-century local farmer) was known as one of the great breadbaskets of the lower Hudson Valley. Later, the rich and famous started their migration north out of Manhattan seeking fresh air and relaxation. Many notable mansions still dot the local landscape, some of them with fascinating pasts.

Felix Warburg (1871–1937) was a multimillionaire financier who was a major patron of the arts (ballet, mostly) and built enormous homes in several places. His five-hundred-acre Hartsdale estate, Woodlands, was the site of many lavish parties and social events, and eventually was deeded to the town for a school. In 1944, his widow donated their mansion on Fifth Avenue in New York City for use as the present Jewish Museum of New York City.

Henry J. Gaisman, a millionaire inventor who ran the Gillette razor company after founder King Gillette died, bought huge tracts of prime land along Ridge Road in Hartsdale, and in 1952, at the age of eighty-two, moved into a mansion there with his much younger first wife (a former nun, age thirty-three). Expecting to die soon, he announced that he was leaving his sprawling estate to the Archdiocese of New York after his death as a home for elderly nuns. He died in 1974 at the ripe old age of 104! Catholic nuns still retire to his former Hartsdale home.

In the 1930s, a clever Greek immigrant named Tom Carvelas opened up his first roadside ice cream store here; the first of what would become hundreds of Carvel Ice Cream Stands. Tom Carvel's inaugural store stood for years at the spot on Central Avenue where he got a flat tire while delivering ice cream and then decided to stay and build an ice cream shop there. In August 2007, the present owner announced the closing of the original Carvel Ice Cream Store to make room for a strip mall. Cookie Pusses all over the Northeast mourned the passing.

Hartsdale is also the home of America's first and largest pet cemetery.

THE MEMORIAL

Starting in 1896 in a rural, remote apple orchard, Hartsdale Pet Cemetery (www
.petcem.com) is now the eternal home of more than seventy-five thousand furry
(and other) friends. Dr. Samuel Johnson, New York's first official veterinarian,
offered his vacation orchard as the final resting place of deceased pets of his cus-
tomers. Little did he know of the future demand for cemetery space. After a newspaper article highlighted this funeral place for dogs, Johnson incorporated the
Hartsdale Canine Cemetery on May 14, 1914. Today, thousands of animals are
buried here in what is called "the Peaceable Kingdom," and everyday household
mutts and stray cats (and even a lion cub) share burial space with the pampered
pets of millionaires and celebrities.

Among the famous stars that have trusted their beloved pets to the perpet-
ual care of Hartsdale Pet Cemetery are Diana Ross, Kate Smith, Robert Merrill,
Mariah Carey, Elizabeth Arden, Joe Garagiola, New York Mayor Jimmy Walker,
Gene Krupa, and others.

Most of the gravestones are small and similar. Most carry just the pet's name
and date of death, and maybe a line or two of comfort written by the owner. Two
graves stand out, however, for their grandiose style, elaborate design, and exces-
sive cost. In the early 1900s, a grieving pet owner named Mrs. M. F. Walsh of New
York City erected a behemoth of a tomb for her beloved dog who would (according to the epitaph chiseled on the side of the fifty-ton marble monument) "lick
the hand that had no food to offer." In 2005, the LaMura family built a massive
above-ground marble mausoleum for their dog Sandy, who was still very much
alive at the completion of the tomb. The entire tribute to Sandy weighs 1,500
pounds and cost $50,000 to erect.

The War Dog Memorial, erected in 1923 at a cost of $2,500, is a touching
tribute to the canine heroes of all wars (although it was initially intended to be
a memorial just to those who served in World War I). The ten-foot high, ten-ton
memorial is made of the highest quality Vermont granite. Sculptor Robert Cater-
son's creation shows a German Shepherd, rigid and on alert, scanning the landscape for (perhaps) a fallen soldier. Draped over his back is a Red Cross blanket, and
at the dog's feet are a military helmet (with a bullet hole in it) and a canteen. It is
truly a heroic work of art. An American flag flying overhead is the perfect finishing
touch to one of the most unusual and eloquent public memorials I have ever seen.

The inscription on the boulder upon which the dog stands guard reads:

Dedicated to the memory of The War Dog. Erected by public contribution by dog lovers. To Man's most faithful friend for the valiant services rendered in the World War of 1914 to 1918.

On the day I was at the Hartsdale Pet Cemetery, the flowers were blooming and the cemetery was in excellent condition. I took note of the stones scattered around the base of the War Dog Memorial. They were fascinating tributes to heroic dogs from all generations. One read, "To Kerry: Died September 29, 1942. Mascot of Fire Department Ladder Co. 29. In memory of Kerry, who made the supreme sacrifice and whose life story, Kerry, the Fire Engine Dog, has entertained many generations of children." Another small stone said, "In memory of the millions of animals whose lives are taken for medical research and testing." Directly under the American flag was a stone which read: "To Robby: Died 2001. Devoted Military Dog. The inspiration of America's First War Dog Retirement Law." Two recent disasters were remembered too. One said, "To Sirius, a heroic canine, and to all who lost their lives in the terrorist attack on the World Trade Center on September 11, 2001." Another one went back even farther in time, "Dedicated to the trainers and their canines who so nobly served as part of the FEMA task force Urban Search and Rescue mission in Oklahoma City in April, 1995."

To reach the War Dog Memorial, simply enter Hartsdale Pet Cemetery at the main gate on Central Avenue and proceed straight to the center of the cemetery. You can't miss it.

Note: There is a back entrance you can use to drive into the cemetery. However, use the Central Avenue entrance. You will have to park along the edge of busy Central Avenue, but you can walk into the cemetery and directly to the War Dog Memorial quickly from this point. The first pet grave you will pass, on your left, is the above-mentioned Sandy. The War Dog Memorial can be seen from the road here.

WHILE HERE

After visiting Hartsdale Pet Cemetery, and while you are still in a mood to "go digging," visit the sprawling Ferncliff Cemetery at 280 Secor Road, Hartsdale (http://www.ferncliffcemetery.com), just a mile or so away. This is the final resting place of dozens of Hollywood stars and famous people of all walks of life. You can obtain a map of the famous burial locations at the front office. Ed Sullivan, Malcolm X, Paul Robeson, Toots Shor, Basil Rathbone, Thelonius Monk, Jim Henson, Joan Crawford, and Madame Chiang Kai-Shek are just a few of the many notables found at Ferncliff. Judy Garland's mausoleum (Unit 9, Alcove HH, Crypt 31) is by far the most sought-out grave here.

REFERENCE FILE

An all encompassing Internet Web site dedicated to war dogs is at http://www .war-dogs.com. Here you can learn of the history of canines in combat, buy books and DVD documentaries, and participate in an organization dedicated to honoring these courageous animals.

30

THREE DAYS OF PEACE AND MUSIC
Woodstock Concert Monument, Bethel

THE PLACE

Bethel, New York, is located in Sullivan County. After decades of struggles, the region is now on the cusp of prosperity and is one of the fastest growing counties in the entire state. Hulking remnants of the giant Borscht Belt hotels and Jewish summer camps from the 1940s and 1950s are rapidly being replaced in the area by the expensive second homes of New York City dwellers. With this influx comes new shopping and dining opportunities, growing communities, a casino, and a new, revitalized tax base. Still overwhelmingly rural in nature, Sullivan County sports green mountains, lush meadows, and cool, clean lakes to lure summer visitors. In 1969, however, it was a lot more than clean lakes that caused Bethel's population to swell from a sleepy crossroads of 2,000 to a pulsating, gyrating gypsy colony of a half million strong (making it, for three days, the second largest city in the state after New York City).

The Woodstock Music Festival is a misnomer. The original site of the concert event was to be in the town of Woodstock, in Ulster County, but fear of an overwhelming crowd caused the good folks of Woodstock to veto the idea. Next up was the town of Wallkill. Amid a rising tide of opposition during this turbulent period, they also blocked the concert. Just weeks before the concert's organizers were planning to cancel the whole idea entirely, Max Yasgur's cow field in Bethel was offered up as a final option. The deal was sealed, and the Woodstock Music Festival would be held in Bethel, some forty miles away from Woodstock!

Concert planners had expected, under ideal weather conditions, no more than two hundred thousand young people to attend this one-time-only event. By the time the numbers were added up, more than a half million half-dressed,

half-stoned, free-spirited, free-love flower children had made the pilgrimage to by now the most famous alfalfa field in America. Between the time that folk singer Richie Havens opened the show with "Minstrel from Gault" at 5:07 pm on Friday, August 15, to the time that Jimi Hendrix closed the show with "Hey Joe" at noon on Monday, August 18, hundreds of thousands of concert-goers had crashed the event ("Hey, man, it's a free concert!"), the New York Thruway was temporarily closed due to bumper-to-bumper traffic, three people died, two babies were born, two babies were miscarried, unknown numbers of "Woodstock babies" were conceived, dozens of drug overdoses were treated, and perhaps the finest array of rock musicians that will ever be in one place at one time had sung to the adulation of the throngs.

Joan Baez was mesmerizing ("We Shall Overcome"), Canned Heat was wild ("Going Up the Country"), Credence Clearwater Revival was a crowd favorite ("Proud Mary"), Melanie was the eternal flower child ("Beautiful People"), Joe Cocker was stunning ("With a Little Help from My Friends"), and the performances of Jimi Hendrix, the Who, Janis Joplin, and Crosby, Stills, Nash, and Young are still considered to be among the finest moments in the history of rock and roll.

Peace, music, and good times ruled the hills of this bucolic town that summer of love in 1969. Today, some four decades later, aging hippies (and others) still loyally make the trek to Bethel to "stop by the garden" once more to pay tribute to a moment in time in America, albeit a brief time, that we almost certainly will never see again.

THE MONUMENT

The good news is that, for the most part, the natural setting of the 1969 Woodstock concert remains intact and well cared for. The huge open "bowl" where hundreds of thousands sat shoulder to shoulder in the rain to hear the performers is today a lush, rolling, manicured green space, far different than the brown, mud-soaked field of August 1969. The area is groomed and fenced off to all traffic other than pedestrian use. The famous stage area can still be delineated. The creeks where nude bathers frolicked still meander along the edges of the concert site. Max Yasgur's farm can still be seen in the distance (it has been the site of a recurring series of "Woodstock revivals" of varying degrees of success). A new entertainment hall sits atop the hillside, and period art exhibits dot the landscape (a totem pole in the center of the field features the likenesses of Jimi Hendrix, Janis Joplin, and Jerry Garcia).

The bad news is that in its cleaned up version, the Woodstock concert venue is almost unrecognizable as anything but a pasture. It is supremely challenging for younger visitors to ever comprehend, looking out at the exquisite beauty of this place, what really happened here. To this end, it is well advised for the casual visitor to pull off at the parking area of the Woodstock Monument, and if no one else is around, to wait a few moments for the next group of visitors to appear (they come by, especially in the summer, at a fairly regular pace). This gives you the opportunity to perhaps be there when a person who was at the 1969 concert comes by and tells his or her tales. It happens a lot (remember, there were a *half million* of them!) as aging members of the Woodstock audience come by to share memories with children and grandchildren. These impromptu discussions are always worth the wait.

The Woodstock Concert Monument is a series of colorful plaques embedded in an enormous block of concrete. The sculpture was created by artist Wayne C. Saward. It is located in the northeast corner of the original concert field. A pathway encircles it and a parking pull-off for several cars is adjacent. Two of the plaques list the names of the entire music lineup of the concert. A larger plaque gives the dates of the festival (August 15, 16, and 17, 1969) and the names of the then-landowners who paid for the marker, Louis, Nicky, and June Gelish. A third multicolored portion of the sculpture features a three-dimensional depiction of the iconic Woodstock logo, originally created by artist Arnold Skolnick. The dove sitting on the guitar neck (representing peace and music) has been called one of the most recognizable logos of the past fifty years.

The monument is situated so as to offer an excellent photo op of the entire concert setting behind it.

To reach the Woodstock Monument (and concert site) take exit 104 of NYS 17, travel NYS 17B eleven miles west, and turn right on Hurd Road. Go to the intersection of West Shore Road and you will see the monument.

WHILE HERE

The Museum at Bethel Woods: An Interpretation of the 1969 Woodstock Music and Arts Fair recently opened at this site. Its role will be to act as a central location for "all things Woodstock." They will also offer guided walking tours of the concert site (http://www.bethelwoodscenter.org). The new concert hall, Bethel Woods Center for the Arts, featured recently, to much fanfare and emotion, a concert starring Crosby, Stills, Nash, and Young. They performed to a crowd of over sixteen thousand fans on August 13, 2006, thirty-seven years to the day from their 1969 appearance at the very same place.

In 1970, the movie *Woodstock* was released to great acclaim and financial success (it won the Academy Award for Best Documentary Feature). Among the

120 miles of footage shot over the long Woodstock weekend to make this film (it was edited by Martin Scorcese), some of the more recognizable places and people have disappeared. Only Hector's Bar, a favorite hippie watering hole for decades, still welcomes patrons much as it did in the summer of 1969, just a mile from the concert venue.

Featured prominently in the movie is Art Vassmer, "Mr. Woodstock," who passed away a few years back. Universally beloved for his kindness to the young invaders of 1969, Vassmer's grocery store in Kauneonga Lake, a mile from the concert site, housed the "Woodstock Museum" for years. He once said that he accepted more than 250 personal checks from the cash-challenged youth of the Woodstock army during the concert and that not a single check bounced! A faded collection of posters, photos, and cheesy memorabilia, the "by donation" museum, attached to his store, still evoked warm memories from passersby and visitors from around the country right up until his death.

My friend from Scotland, Cameron Oliver, and I were making one of our frequent pilgrimages to Woodstock recently, and we planned our usual first stop at Vassmer's place. When we pulled up in front of the rickety old store, we noticed the front door was wide open, but the lights were turned off. We yelled inside and a voice hollered back, "We're closed. The store is out of business." We walked around back and noticed helpers piling the store contents (mostly picked-over junk) into the back of a truck. It was like someone was ripping out a piece of our hearts! Cameron and I asked if we could take something, anything, as a reminder of this old, nostalgic place. They told us, "Sure, but there ain't much left." We both grabbed a couple of "Keys Made Here" signs and left. We are convinced that Art Vassmer must have made some keys for the throng that came here that weekend in 1969. At least we *want* to believe that!

The old store, like Mr. Woodstock, is a distant memory now.

REFERENCE FILE

Countless books and articles have been written about the 1969 Woodstock concert. New titles hit the bookstore shelves each year. Though the DVD of the concert from 1970 stands as the ultimate Woodstock Baedeker, the book *The Road to Woodstock* by Michael Lang (ECCO Publishing, 2010) is an interesting look at the event from the inside. Lang was a co-creator of the concert.

WHO SAYS PUBLIC ART CAN'T BE FUN?

Meet the Roosevelts, Hyde Park

The thirty-first (and bonus) entry in this book belongs to one of the most popular pieces of public art anywhere in the state. I included it in this book to show that all monuments, statues, or memorials don't have to be serious, heady, deep, somber remembrances.

Located at FDR's home (Springwood) in Hyde Park, New York, this stunning double statue of Franklin and Eleanor Roosevelt sits in a small plaza near the Henry A. Wallace Visitor and Education Center (Wallace was one of FDR's vice presidents) at this historic site. It is almost impossible to pass these two legends without joining in on their little park-bench tête-à-tête. Both are dressed formally, he in a business suit, she in a dress, but they look perfectly natural sitting outside in this gorgeous setting of his ancestral home. A small reading table separates them, as Eleanor enjoys an afternoon cup of tea and the president catches up on the daily newspapers. They are both smiling, as if enjoying a private little joke between them.

This statue, sculpted by StudioEIS Bronzeworks of Brooklyn—Elliot and Ivan Schwartz, with the help of a team of twenty artists—is finite to the most exacting degree, from FDR's strong hands to Eleanor's toothy grin and her wispy, coiffed hairdo. It is no wonder this bronze depiction of two of the twentieth century's most familiar personalities took more than six months to complete. The artists cleverly left a space on the bench next to President Roosevelt, and hundreds have enjoyed plopping down next to him, throwing their arm around the

great man's neck, and mugging for the camera. It must be the most photographed statue in this book!

The FDR Library is one of the top three visited presidential libraries in the nation. Thousands make the trek to this wondrous Hudson River landmark every year, including busloads of schoolchildren. I have been there several times myself, and it is always fun to watch the kids (and the grandparents) giggle as they approach Franklin and Eleanor and pose for a picture with the First Couple. This double statue is clearly made for the young and the young at heart. Children born long after the New Deal still get a kick out of being with the Roosevelts.

The two in the photo above, our littlest ones Abby and Joey, are proof that *public art can be fun!!*